MANAGING THE IMPACT OF POLITICAL
CRISES ON TOURISM

blood on the beach

Vorawan Kanlayanasukho | Patrice Veuthey

MANAGING THE IMPACT OF POLITICAL CRISES ON TOURISM

blood on the beach

Vorawan Kanlayanasukho | Patrice Veuthey

Mereo Books

1A The Wool Market Dyer Street Cirencester Gloucestershire GL7 2PR
An imprint of Memoirs Publishing www.mereobooks.com

Blood on the Beach: 978-1-86151-307-6

First published in Great Britain in 2016
by Mereo Books, an imprint of Memoirs Publishing

Copyright ©2016

The address for Memoirs Publishing Group Limited can be found at
www.memoirspublishing.com

The Memoirs Publishing Group Ltd Reg. No. 7834348

The Memoirs Publishing Group supports both The Forest Stewardship Council®
(FSC®) and the PEFC® leading international forest-certification organisations. Our
books carrying both the FSC label and the PEFC® and are printed on FSC®-certified
paper. FSC® is the only forest-certification scheme supported by the leading
environmental organisations including Greenpeace. Our paper procurement policy
can be found at www.memoirspublishing.com/environment

Typeset in 10/14pt Century Schoolbook
by Wiltshire Associates Publisher Services Ltd. Printed and bound in Great Britain
by Printondemand-Worldwide, Peterborough PE2 6XD

ABOUT THE AUTHORS

Dr Vorawan Kanlayanasukho was awarded a doctorate in tourism by Manchester Metropolitan University in 2013 for her research on political crises management for the tourism industry. A native of Thailand, she is also the founder of AyaThai Travel, an integrated travel services provider serving mainly corporate and government markets.

Patrice Veuthey is a Swiss executive with a long industry experience in aviation, leisure and travel on three continents, and has a keen grasp of regional sociocultural differences and crisis resolution. He is currently managing director of the AyaThai Group subsidiaries in Europe.

ABOUT VORAWAN & ASSOCIATES LTD.

Vorawan & Associates is a tourism crisis management consultancy based in London. The practice relies upon academics and professionals to provide effective solutions based on sound theory and real-world experience.

CONTENTS

PREFACE

This book is partially derived from my PhD thesis 'Development Of A Framework Of Political Crisis Responses For The Tourism Industry', published in 2013, with a greater emphasis on the application side drawn from the real-life business experience of my co-author, Patrice Veuthey, and myself. It seems more useful and applicable to present the material in a readily accessible form for people to whom its findings will be interesting and useful, notably those employed in the tourism industry and industry stakeholders.

References to events and crises that have occurred since the original research also supplement the original material. The first chapter is devoted to the terror attack on the beaches of Tunisia because of its significance for the tourism industry at large: it was more than a destination being affected, it was the product itself - the beach – that was at the heart of the crisis.

The Brussels lockdown following the November 2015 terror attack in Paris transformed a destination crisis event into a product crisis affecting all major cities. With the US State Department having issued a worldwide travel alert a few days later, tourism stakeholders face the broadest threat to the industry since the last world war as its key products, beaches and major cities, are affected globally by current events.

We hope that our book will be helpful in your endeavours.

V Kanlayanasukho
January 2016

ACKNOWLEDGEMENTS

A great many people shared their experience and contributed knowledge towards the research leading to my thesis which became the foundation of this book, and accordingly I would like to thank them.

First, my doctoral supervisors – Professor Howard Hughes, Dr Amanda Miller, Dr Shobana Nair Partington and Dr Steven Rhoden. Their patience, support and invaluable help and encouragement led me through the completion of my thesis.

Many others have supported and influenced the direction of the past six years of research and study, first toward the thesis and then leading to the publication of this book. The continued encouragement and help of Professor Philip L. Pearce from James Cook University, the assistance of Wattana Watjanakomkul during the interview phase, the professional advice of Nick James of The Air Travel Consultancy who is partly responsible for the idea of deriving a practical business book from the academic thesis.

Above all, I want to express my warmest thanks to my family for their unconditional loving support and so much more. A special thanks to my brother, Puttichai; he was my first English teacher, my earliest idol and always supported me. Thank you also to my sister, Tippawan, for being my closest friend and confidante, always offering love and support. Many thanks to my husband, Piyapong Chitchumnong and my son, August, who inspired me to complete the final publishing process.

Last but not least, a very special thank you to Patrice Veuthey for supporting and assisting me throughout the process, by challenging my opinions and conclusions and establishing and maintaining a solid foundation for both the theory behind the thesis and its application derived in this book. Then Patrice drove the process of completing this book by updating and summarising content from the original thesis and writing additional chapters to broaden its value and appeal to the business sector of tourism and casual readers alike.

INTRODUCTION

Political crises unfolding in or near tourist destinations can have a devastating effect, far beyond the human tragedy which is often the immediate result. The repercussions of these events affect many people and organisations, from the innocent holidaymaker to local political bodies and tourism organisations. They may ruin industries, cities, even countries. So learning to manage them and their after-effects is vital.

Disruptions caused by political crises such as the September 11 2001 attacks, the Bali bombing of 2002 and 2005, the Arab Spring beginning in 2010 and the chronic Thai political crises originating as far back as 1932 and unresolved to this day, have drawn attention to the effects of political crises on tourism and prompted scholars to research the subject. While there are several studies of tourism crises caused by terrorism and natural disasters, few in-depth studies have explored the impact on the tourism industry of political crises in general. This book is an attempt to redress the balance by applying crisis management to political crises and provide a framework for political crisis responses and practical solutions for the tourism industry.

The effects of political crises upon tourism organisations fall into two categories: direct impact, which includes the perception effect, the financial effect and the aftermath, and indirect impact, which includes the coinciding effect, ripple effect and spillover effect, as I will explain later.

Tourists' perception of a crisis and its effects can severely damage the image of a destination, and that image is critical to its economic success or failure. My research brought to light the significance of different sources of crisis information as well as shaping the political crisis classification model offered in this book.

The model and the framework of responses and solutions should help the tourism industry understand the dynamics involved and how to manage each phase effectively. The primary focus has been placed on crisis management responses to make this book a practical guide for tourism stakeholders.

There is no doubt that political crises inflict much more rapid and much greater damage on affected destinations than in the past, because of faster communication and the rise of social media. Since the turn of the century, internet communications such as social networks and online media have become ubiquitous communication channels for business and consumers alike overshadowing the dominance of traditional media. Local and remote events alike are exposed faster, and to a far greater number of people, than ever before.

New channels of communication have greatly diversified the sources of information tourists rely upon. As social media communities, news organisations and users have converged in social media spaces, they can and do respond instantly to sudden events. Consequently, news of political crises and their effects has become both faster and easier to obtain. For example, a tourist who witnessed Thai protests in Bangkok in 2010 could take a video and immediately upload it to social media or email it to their friends. In the world of instant communications, political crises are magnified to the world; the way the crisis is managed by a destination, as it unfolds, immediately affects both its image and organisational confidence towards it. This means political crises have much greater consequences than in the past.

Secondly, there is an increasing economic disparity between developed and developing countries. The growing income inequality within these countries significantly contributes to their instability. Poverty, increasing government debt, exploding populations and inadequate living standards all help to fuel local wars, ethnic and religious conflicts and even regional arms races. There is much literature documenting how economic or societal crises can lead such states to political crises.

Countering the effects of political crises requires close collaboration between tourism stakeholders. Trade organisations need a framework and clear guidelines to help them to navigate their way through the phases of a crisis.

CHAPTER 1

THE DAY THE BEACH
FELL TO TERRORISM

The beach is the iconic image of vacation and the most sought-after inspiration for leisure and relaxation. It is also the most frequently-featured image to entice consumers to go on a holiday. The beach is synonymous with carefree time away from the realities of the world, the place where one can escape barefoot and wearing little clothing.

Unlike other tourist attractions which are usually well patrolled by security forces, beaches are frequently only protected by lifeguards from the dangers of the water, not that of the sand. Beachgoers are exposed in bare open spaces with few if any structures for protection and by the nature of the location with typically only one escape path. In military terms, the beach is a soft target, a very big one with very many people spread over a very large area, making it very difficult to keep it secure. Yet there is no feeling of insecurity, as in no one's mind is the image of the beach associated with violence, let alone terrorism.

It is that psychological effect of a violent event in a peaceful and security unencumbered location that makes the beach a desirable target when the intent is to cause fear and disruption rather than control or destruction.

At midday on June 26 2015, a lone gunman arrived on the beach of Port El Kantaoui, just north of Sousse in Tunisia, and opened fire on the tourists on the beach with an assault rifle. He then entered the lobby of the Riu Imperial Marhaba hotel, where he may have thrown an explosive device, then returned to the beach heading north in front of the Riu Bellevue Park hotel and turned into a small street connecting the beach with the main road, where he was killed by police. In the span of about an hour, the 23-year old Tunisian student had killed 38 foreigners and injured 39 others, including seven Tunisians. Sousse being a popular tourist destination in Great Britain, most of the victims, 55 in total, were British holidaymakers. Within hours of the attack, ISIS claimed responsibility by publishing a picture of the gunman with weapons next to him.

The terror attack on the beach of Sousse in Tunisia on 26 June 2015 suddenly changed that perception of safety, as it brought a great loss of lives among tourists and occurred in an area assumed safe even as other areas of the country may not have been. In the case of Tunisia, it had already suffered a terrorist attack at another popular tourist destination, the Bardo Museum in Tunis.

With extensive media coverage, particularly in the UK, of the trauma of blood on the beach in a destination especially popular with British tourists, public uncertainty about beach resorts and holiday destinations located in regions affected by ideological or political violence is likely to increase, in contrast to the diminishing effects generally experienced after violent events in other types of tourist destinations. Unlike site-specific terror attacks such as that in Luxor in Egypt, or the Bardo Museum in Tunis a few months earlier, or even the beach resort in Kenya, the Sousse event is likely to affect the perception of all beach destinations in regions susceptible to terror attacks. Even seemingly unrelated political crises could further magnify that perception, as in the case of Greece, where some European tourists may fear that the economic crisis could lead to violent acts against them.

On 9 July, several days after the Sousse attack, the British Foreign and Commonwealth Office (FCO) changed its notice for Tunisia to advise against all but essential travel to the entire country. The significance of the travel advisory update is that it was issued nearly two weeks after the occurrence. The FCO is rarely slow to react to events and is always well aware of the consequences its advisories may cause. The FCO had evidently received intelligence that another such attack was likely to occur again in the near future and that the situation in Tunisia warranted the change in its advisory. British operators closely follow FCO advisories, mainly because travel insurance coverage is no longer available once the FCO advise against travel to a destination. This effectively shut down all of Tunisia as a tourist destination in the British market.

Comparing the impact on tourism of the earlier Bardo museum attack in Tunis in March with the Sousse beach attack in June shows significant differences, even though both attacks shared many similarities: one or two gunmen, likely from the same terrorist group, armed with automatic weapons specifically targeting tourists, similar numbers of casualties among the tourists, and both concluding with the gunmen killed by police. But the aftermath was very different. The media coverage and reactions from abroad to the museum attack were predictable and comparable to that of past terrorist attacks on tourists, but the intensity of media coverage of the beach attack was far greater and longer lasting, due in part to the fact that the bodies of the British victims were repatriated by the Royal Air Force, providing further visual reminders of the event and underlining the importance given to the attack by the UK government. Further, the upgraded British FCO travel advisory on Tunisia coming out nearly two weeks after the events raised again the visibility and awareness of the attack in the British media.

The other important difference was the location of these attacks. Where the museum is a physical location now stigmatized by terrorism, it is not a sweeping and generic identification of Tunisia as a tourism destination. On the other hand, the beach in Sousse is now known as "the beach" in Tunisia, the very core of tourism for many tourism destinations. The mention of a discrete location like the museum can be easily avoided in the tourism recovery process, but any effort to downplay the beach would remove the most important selling point of that destination. In addition, the breach of trust of the safety traditionally associated with beach vacations renders any attempt to regain consumer confidence a very difficult and time-consuming task.

OTHER BEACH ATTACKS

Sousse was not the first time that a terror attack had taken place on or near a beach targeting tourists. In October 2013, just a few kilometres south of the June 2015 attack, a man blew himself up on the beach in front of the Ryadh hotel, also located in Sousse, in a failed attempt. While there were no other casualties in this incident, it was covered in the media, particularly in the British press.

Other violent events targeting tourists on or near a beach include:

In the early morning of 11 September 2011, five men raided the luxury beach resort of Kiwayu, killing one British guest and abducting his wife. This exclusive resort is one of the most expensive in Kenya, but it is located just a few kilometres from the Somali border. Somali Islamists frequently attack locals in the vicinity and it could be assumed that such an exclusive resort had security to match, but there was no clash during the raid and the abductors were able to leave by boat undetected. The hostage was released six months later, probably after a ransom had been paid. This incident had no effect on tourism in Kenya for several reasons. It took place in a very remote location, not at a popular destination; also, there were no other tourists at the resort at the time, which aside from explaining the single casualty, is probably the main reason for the limited media exposure, as no one on location gave it visibility on social media. The fact that it was not a terrorist attack per se but a ransom-seeking attack, even if the attackers were most likely elements of the al-Shabaab terrorist organization, also diminished the fear factor effect.

In the early evening of 1st October 2005, two bombs exploded at the beach restaurants on Jimbaran Beach in Bali, which is popular with tourists, mainly Australians at this time of the year. A short while later, another bomb exploded in a restaurant in Kuta town square. Three unexploded bombs were later found at the beach restaurants of Jimbaran Beach. The total casualties for all sites were 20 deaths and 129 injured, including a large number of tourists. While the bombs were small compared to the first Bali bombing, they contained shrapnel and exploded among the diners, causing severe injury within a smaller perimeter. Also, five bombs had been planted at beach restaurants. It appear that three suicide bombers conducted the attack, two at the beach and one at the town centre. The bombing was probably conducted by Jemaah Islamiah, the same terrorist group responsible for the 2002 Bali bombing and other bombings in Indonesia in 2003 and 2004. Bali tourism had barely recovered from the 2002 terrorist attack and the renewed terrorism on the island was extensively covered in the world media. However by 2007 tourism had recovered and the highest number of international arrivals was recorded.

On the night of 23 July 2005, the deadliest terrorist attack in Egypt's recent history caused 88 deaths, including more than 20 foreign tourists. It took place in the popular tourist destination of Sharm el-Sheikh. Two car bombs, one at the Old Market and one at the Ghazala hotel, caused most of the casualties. The third bomb, hidden in a bag on the beachside walkway, killed seven tourists and one Egyptian. A terrorist group linked to Al-Qaeda claimed responsibility for the attack.

With about a third of the total number of hotel rooms in Egypt, Sharm el-Sheikh is critically important to Egyptian tourism. The destination's recovery also suffered from the successive political crises in Egypt in addition to the difficulty of recovering from a terrorist attack at a beach resort. Being remote from the main tourist attractions, Luxor and the Pyramids, which still suffer from the stigma of terrorism attached to them, Sharm el-Sheikh had been able to compete effectively with the likes of beach resorts in Spain and Italy due to its lower prices until 2005. In the following decade, although the resort did recover somewhat, this was negatively affected by other events in Egypt.

On the night of 7 October 2004, a truck loaded with explosive destroyed the Taba Hilton in Ras al-Shitan, Egypt, killing 31

people and injuring 159 others. Two other bombs exploded near
the Moon Island Resort and the Baddiyah camp on the beach
killing 3 more people and injuring 12. About half of the dead
were foreign tourists, mostly Israeli. Ras al-Shitan was a
popular beach destination for Israeli until the October 2004
bombing. The Israeli tourists did not come back, and the much
smaller number of European and Egyptian tourists does not
make up for the loss.

KILLING FOREIGN TOURISTS IS ONLY A MEANS TO ACHIEVE THE TERRORISTS' OBJECTIVES

Traditionally, ideological or militant terrorist groups attempt to
cause as many casualties as possible to destabilize the social
order and cause disruption and anxiety among the population.
However, larger terrorist organizations, such as Al-Qaeda in the
past and more recently ISIS, with goals of greater scope, have
defined complex strategies that may differ significantly from
those of historical militant groups. At times, their tactics may
even seem to conflict with their objectives. For example, they
may seek to keep casualties low among the local population so
as to avoid a backlash that could nullify the potential gain of
sympathy of the local men and women most likely to be
receptive to the ideology of the organization. In the Sousse
attack, the lone gunman did not attack the Tunisian workers
who blocked his way toward the second beach chair area;
instead he ran around them.

An attack on tourists at the beach aims at disrupting the
economy by specifically targeting tourism at its most visible and
most sensitive point: the beach. The media impact of blood on
the beach will leave a more vivid and lasting impression on the
audience than that of the charred ruins of a blown-up hotel. It
is also likely to cause fewer casualties among local workers than

within a hotel or resort, and far fewer than in a market (as seen in the 2005 Bali bombing where most casualties were local men and women at the market area). In a country like Tunisia, where tourism contributes upwards of 15% of GDP and employs one out of every seven Tunisian workers, the Sousse attack and the subsequent British FCO travel advisory encompassing the entire country is as economically damaging as that of a major earthquake. The difference is that no relief and economic support is forthcoming from abroad, as would be the case after a natural disaster.

The ultimate objective is to drive enrolment into the organization by demoralizing the population through economic disruption, resulting in rising unemployment and poverty. The weak and the disenchanted can then be more easily lured into the organization, particularly among the country's youth. Tunisia was already a prime recruiting ground for ISIS, with Tunisians making up the largest contingent of foreign fighters in Syria. At the southern border with Libya it is also difficult to control the movement of people, militants and weapons in and out of the region.

A NEW PROBLEM OF TOURISM CRISIS MANAGEMENT

The Sousse beach attack creates a new type of problem for tourism crisis management, that of a threat and a potential crisis with the product itself – the beach – rather than with a defined destination. As the likelihood of another terrorist attack on another beach in the region or elsewhere in the world is likely greater than another attack in Sousse, which will no doubt benefit from increased security, the larger challenge becomes to restore and preserve the image of the product, as other beach destinations may be potentially perceived as unsafe.

As tourism crisis recoveries always originate with the

affected destination, there is little experience and few examples of campaigns and strategies from the originating markets to recover the trust in a tourism product affected by fear of insecurity rather than a destination. However the framework and strategies laid out in this book are just as applicable to such situations as they are for traditional tourism destination recoveries, as they originate from the broad academic theory of crisis recovery.

CHAPTER 2

HOW POLITICAL CRISES DAMAGE TOURISM

The success or failure of tourist destinations depends first and foremost on their ability to convey an image of a safe and secure environment for visitors. A country experiencing a political crisis, particularly if there is military action, can expect a rapid decline in the number of foreign visitors – and it is likely to be a long time before they return, even after the trouble has gone away.

As political crises become more frequent through growing economic disparities and ideological extremism fuelled by income and social inequality, they also become much more visible, far more rapidly. Media communication, transformed by the digital age, brings instant news and pictures of trouble to the attention of the public across the world. Recent events such as the prolonged protests in Thailand, the recurring crises stemming from the Arab Spring or the more recent crisis in

Ukraine call for effective crisis management strategies capable of rapid and effective responses.

When terrorists bombed the island paradise of Bali in 2002, the attacks 'ripped the heart out of the island's tourism industry' (www.eturbonews.com), leaving over half the population unemployed. The crisis exposed shortcomings in security, medical infrastructure and emergency management, which further damaged the island's image and made the recovery process much more difficult. The first crisis phase stretched right up to the time of the second bombing in 2005, in part because the Indonesian government was slow to embrace recovery. But the second bombing, rather than delaying recovery, prompted the government to react. As a result, the island had climbed back to its previous 2001 peak by 2007 and enjoyed high growth rates from 2008 onwards.

In this strife-torn world crises like this are not new, nor are they unusual. Looking back over 30 years, in 1983 the Sri Lankan Civil War ended ten years of growth for a popular tourism destination. It was only after the end of the civil war, in 2009, that tourism growth resumed in earnest. Later in this book, when we look at the effects of political crises on alternative destinations, we will see how the Thai tourism industry somewhat unwittingly benefited from the Sri Lankan crisis.

The magnitude of the loss of tourists through political crises is best exemplified by Syria. In 2010 there were 8.5 million tourists, comparable to that of Switzerland or Japan. A few years later almost all of them had gone, never to return. That is an even bigger fall than Egypt suffered over the same period.

Not all crises damage tourism. In a few instances a crisis well-handled turns into an opportunity that ultimately benefits the tourism industry. Such was the case with the Thai government's handling of the 2004 tsunami, although it can be argued that as this was a natural disaster, apolitical by its very nature, it was possible to adopt a more straightforward and less compromised response strategy.

Political crises don't just shift tourist flows for the months following the event – they leave the affected destination suffering long after the crisis has abated, thanks to the negative image that has been created. For crisis management in these cases to be effective, careful planning is required.

REGIONAL EFFECTS

As crises tend to affect more than the destination which has been directly affected, our scope includes the surrounding regions which also suffer, even indirectly from a neighbouring crisis.

Tourism is a major factor in international relations, and tourism development is often strongly influenced by political implications, sometimes by design but also, at times, by neglect. We have seen in recent years how government policies can at times favour tourism and at other times damage the industry, most often through changes of leadership and political priorities. The United Kingdom is an example. Where political sensitivities about immigration clash with the desire to exploit the economic value of tourists of certain origins, we see inconsistent or intentionally vague visa policies designed to satisfy the needs of some while avoiding the ire of others, as mentioned in the next section.

When political crises occur in emerging countries, the unpredictability and the sudden changes in government attitudes to tourism add to the difficulties of planning crisis management. A recent example of conflicting signals affecting a recovery strategy occurred in Thailand in December 2014 with marketing for the New Year's Eve celebrations. Several travel media had just rated Bangkok among the best places in the world to spend New Year's Eve when a government official announced a ban on the sale of alcohol at New Year. This news was promptly followed by a denial by the Prime Minister's office. As one would expect, the ban made for more coverage in global media than its subsequent denial, leaving doubts in the minds of prospective New Year's Eve tourists and travel agents who did not want to take a chance and preferred to steer their clients to more predictable destinations.

The visa factor is one of the fundamental mechanics used to boost tourism to a particular country. Korea, for instance, is still the major outbound destination market for Thai tourists because of the short distance between the two countries, the availability of low-cost airlines and the absence of visa requirements. Government leaders accordingly perceive tourism as a political bridge between nations. Another important consideration is that tourism politics have been largely overlooked, although relations between individual countries by means of multinational corporations such as hotel chains, airlines, tour companies and credit facilities are of tremendous political importance; many have more financial assets than any other industry in their respective countries. The ramifications of this extend to financing, managing and controlling the tourism industry in such countries.

GOVERNMENTS, PUBLIC SERVICES AND TOURISM

The efficiency of public services has a significant effect on tourism and can be crucial to those destinations which are regularly affected by political crises. Public administration likewise plays a major role in the recovery period in normal circumstances, as crime levels, the friendliness of residents, safe roads and aesthetics all illustrate how well-monitored tourism development can influence tourist satisfaction.

By manipulating visas, currency regulations, internal access and export and import procedures, public policy directly affects tourism and controls the numbers of tourists, as well as their spending. The OECD (2006) advocates a whole-government approach to tourism policy, recognising tourism as a sector that includes a wide range of activities across economic sectors. This involves national and regional levels with many government departments. Within three months of his election as Britain's coalition Prime Minister in 2010, David Cameron spoke of the importance of tourism to the UK's overall economic health:

"For too long tourism has been looked down on as a second-class service sector. That's just wrong. Tourism is a fiercely competitive market, requiring skills, talent, enterprise and a government that backs Britain. It's fundamental to the rebuilding and rebalancing of our economy. It's one of the best and fastest ways of generating the jobs we need so badly in this country. And it's absolutely crucial to us making the most of the Olympics... I want us to have the strongest possible tourism strategy. I think there are four parts. First – what government does nationally. Second – the role of local government and the support of the local area. Third – how we stimulate the private sector in tourism. And fourth – how we make policy in other areas that will impact the tourism industry. I want to have the strongest possible engagement with the tourism industry in each of these areas."

This statement by the British Prime Minister was intended to demonstrate political engagement with tourism. However, this was an example of the situation referred to above, where a government tries to steer a course between two different agendas. Other political decisions regarding immigration taken at about the same time by the same government introduced tougher visa rules which adversely affected tourism and, in effect, negated that engagement with the industry. For example, the recent fast-growing Chinese outbound market had an impact on the public policies of the United Kingdom, such as easing visa regulation for Chinese visitors in order to strengthen the tourism industry. David Cameron again:

"Last year, the UK Border Agency processed almost 300,000 visa applications for Chinese nationals, with 97% of visas processed within 15 days. China is a priority market for the UK, and we want to support both tourists and business people coming to our country... there was an increase in visit visas issued to Chinese nationals of 6% last year. In December, the Home Secretary set out a range of improvements to the visa process, particularly to support business customers, and they will be implemented this year."

The political upheaval in Egypt in 2011 effectively destroyed one of the Mediterranean's most successful and lucrative travel industries. Similarly, the failure of the Thai government to control protesters in 2008 led to Bangkok Airport shutting its doors for several weeks, leading to a severe decline in tourism in the country the following year.

Given the rise in international political conflicts, there is a need to understand these issues in much greater depth.

CHAPTER 3

PROBLEM, CRISIS OR DISASTER?

A crisis is an event that interrupts normal business transactions to the extent of threatening the very existence of an organisation. The Chinese word for crisis is a combination of two words, *wei* and *ji*, meaning 'danger' and 'opportunity', reflecting the idea that a crisis can be a turning point for better as well as for worse. As we'll see later, a crisis can sometimes act to draw tourists in instead of keeping them away. Whether a crisis is viewed as positive or negative will depend on the values associated with the outcome.

The meaning of the word 'disaster' however is less ambiguous. Literally referring to unfavourable heavenly portents – 'bad stars' - the word tends to be applied to any seriously negative event. Examples of defined disasters include the 2004 Indian Ocean earthquake and tsunami and the 2011 Christchurch earthquake. The 2014 Ebola outbreak surely qualified as a disaster in the affected region.

Because of the increased frequency of crisis incidents, the

popularity of the term has seen a dramatic increase in recent decades. The Bhopal tragedy (1984), the Luxor Massacre (1997), the September 11 attacks (2001), the Arab Spring (2010–2011), the Japanese tsunami (2011), the Egypt protests (2011–2013) or the Syrian civil war (2011-present) all clearly deserve the term. It is clear that crisis study warrants the attention of tourism research.

CLASSIFICATION OF CRISES

Crises are commonly classified in two categories: human-induced and naturally occurring. Human-induced crises in turn fall into two kinds, those caused deliberately, as in terrorist attacks, or happening by accident, as with industrial accidents or spillages of pollutants. Examples of the former include the Lockerbie bombing in 1988, the Luxor Massacre in 1997 and the September 11 attacks in 2001, while the Asian financial crisis of 1997 and the Tylenol poisoning in 1982 and the Bhopal industrial accident in 1984 were not deliberate.

It has been argued that industrial crises like Bhopal, in which more than 3000 people died and hundreds of thousands were injured following an accidental release of toxic gas, are the result of organisational, social and political failings – collective human error. Similarly, competitive pressure within business and industry raises the risk of catastrophic human error.

Natural crises, on the other hand, have always afflicted mankind and always will. Natural events outside our control, such as floods, earthquakes, volcanic eruptions, tsunamis and epidemics account on average for more than a million deaths annually around the world while causing major economic loss, social upheaval and other disruption. Recent natural crises include the 2011 earthquake off the Pacific coast of Tohoku, which claimed the lives of 15,883 people; the November 2013 typhoon Yolanda which left over 6,000 people dead in the Philippines; the February 2011 Christchurch earthquake, one of New Zealand's deadliest peacetime disasters, which killed 185 people; and the swine flu pandemic of 2009 and 2010. While not causing death, the 2010 volcanic eruptions of Eyjafjallajokull in Iceland brought major disruption to air travel across western and northern Europe, causing significant economic damage to the aviation and tourism industries.

A particularly notorious human-induced event occurred in Japan in 2011 when a tsunami resulting from an earthquake caused damage to the Fukushima Daiichi Nuclear Power Plant complex and released radioactive gas into the atmosphere. Although the immediate cause of the disaster was natural, the Fukushima Nuclear Accident Independent Investigation Commission found that it was "manmade" and that its direct effects were all foreseeable. The report also found that the plant had been incapable of withstanding the forces released by the earthquake and tsunami. There were more than 15,000 deaths and 6,000 injuries, with many more people missing, to say nothing of losses of tens of billions of dollars.

PHYSICAL (NATURAL) CRISES

Physical crises like earthquakes, devastating as they may be, do not have the lasting social impact associated with political instability, war, civil unrest or terrorist attacks. Tourists appreciate that in most cases, once the disaster has happened, it is over and done with, and that recovery will follow, however slow. The Indonesian tsunami of Boxing Day 2004 killed at least 230,000 people in 14 countries, but within a few years the region had once again become a popular tourist destination.

It is often a different matter for the key area examined by this book - political crises - because the danger is often perceived to continue indefinitely.

POLITICAL CRISES

Political crises emerge from instability – any situation where a régime is subject to unpredictable change and disruption. Political instability can greatly affect a local tourism economy even before it leads to violence. It may be the consequence of an economic or social crisis, as seen in the 1970 riots in Poland, where an economic crisis immediately led to a political one. A commonly accepted academic definition of a political crisis is: "Any sudden or unpredictable incident originated from the country's instability of political institution or of the party system, where its impacts are disruptive to the economy, such as damage to the infrastructure or facilities and loss of life". The consequences are typically negative media coverage, damage to the image of an area, loss of visitor or investor confidence, a decrease in tourist numbers and a resultant loss of revenue and market share.

Clearly not every political crisis is going to damage tourism; the formation of a coalition government in the United Kingdom might have been considered a crisis by those in the corridors of power, but it was never likely to cause the kind of violence or disruption that makes an area unsafe for tourists. However the much more violent events in Thailand in 2010 stemmed from a cause which was in principal similar – an internal conflict between opposing parties.

For the purpose of planning, it is essential to determine when and how political crises affect the tourism industry. In this book we will look in detail at political crises and their impact, and aim to show how important it is for the tourism industry to understand them.

It is important in classifying crises to assess the level of impact, so that appropriate crisis management strategies can be implemented. A number of scholars have attempted to classify different types of political crises. Five basic types were first listed by Lea and Small (1988): wars, coups, terrorism, riots and strikes. An additional type, political unrest, was added by Hall and O'Sullivan (1996). Henderson (2007) suggested further that corruption could be added to the list.

The most commonly-used classification of political instability (Hall and O'Sullivan) appears below. It is applied to various political instability and terrorism studies.

TABLE 3.1 DIMENSIONS OF POLITICAL INSTABILITY

Dimension	Examples
International war	Iraqi invasion of Kuwait had massive impact on international travel.
Civil wars	Sri Lanka Civil War had massive impact on tourism.
Coups	The 2006 and 2014 coups in Thailand had a severe impact on visitor numbers.
Terrorism	The Bali bombings in 2002 and the September attacks in 2011 had severely affected tourism for a longer period.
Riots Political protests Social unrest	Political protests of the Arab Spring in 2011 caused disruption to the tourism industry.
Strikes	The Lufthansa strike in 2012 had substantial impacts on transport networks.

Source: Modified after Hall and O'Sullivan (1996, p. 109)

According to a 2003 study by Dr. David Beirman from Sydney, Australia, crises have been classified in a military context by global armed forces in relation to levels of readiness. The United States Armed Forces classify by defence conditions, known as DEFCON. The scale ascends from DEFCON 5, the lowest state of readiness, up to DEFCON 1 as the situation becomes increasingly severe. DEFCON 1 represents the expectation of an imminent nuclear attack, and has never actually been declared.

David Beirman applied the DEFCON model to his own scale, DESTCON. DESTCON 1, maximum force readiness, would be a crisis with widespread global or regional repercussions on tourism. The September 11 attacks were an example of DESTCON 2 (increased force readiness), which includes widespread terrorism, natural disasters, disease or widespread disorder in which the safety of tourists is under measurable threat. DESTCON 3 (increased force readiness) includes major problems within identifiable regions in the destination, which are well publicised and present a credible threat to tourists in the area. Such events include the Port Arthur Massacre and the Fiji military coup. DESTCON 4 refers to situations that arise during peacetime which warrant increased intelligence and strengthened security measures, including isolated problems within a destination, such as crime or low-level political disturbances. Lastly, DESTCON 5 situations also occur during peacetime and present a minimal perceived threat to a destination.

This approach is of limited use in dealing with political crises because of their unpredictable nature. However the different types of political crisis situations such as coups, strikes, riots and terrorism need be defined clearly, because this can affect management approaches in responding to their effects.

WARS

In the years following World War II, increasing wealth and the development of faster and more efficient modes of transport led to a boom in foreign travel, bringing people to exotic and beautiful places they had never dreamed of visiting before. It also brought many more people into contact with countries and peoples affected by war and political instability.

The 1991-1995 Croatian War of Independence, the Gaza War, the 2006 Lebanon War, the Sri Lankan Civil War and the two Gulf Wars all exemplify how war zones negatively impact tourism.

Wars can be cross-border conflicts, wars of attrition and civil wars. The outbreak of war tends to have a negative impact on tourism in larger areas and for a longer period of time than the war itself. Civil wars are particularly damaging, as a domestic crisis focused within the country can cause greater harm to a destination and its public image than a conflict taking place at the border away from the destination itself (as in Israel). Such was the case with the Sri Lankan Civil War.

Warfare clearly brings disastrous consequences to affected destinations. In addition to the dangers presented to the individual, military activity can damage infrastructure. For example, in the Middle East, years of civil war and conflicts have severely harmed the tourism industry and affected tourism development; the tourism infrastructure, including roads, airports, hotels and restaurants, along with the appeal of the region as a destination, has been largely destroyed by war. In Lebanon, the Lebanese Civil War, lasting from 1975 to 1990, destroyed whole cities and towns. Although Lebanon has gained increasing popularity with tourists since the war ended, tourism there has suffered a new setback from the current Syrian conflict at its border, posing perhaps an even greater new challenge.

Warfare affects a country's long-term economic stability as well as its image as a destination. It is important here to note that war disrupts both sides of the tourism equation - supply and demand. In Zimbabwe, the battle over independence between 1965 and 1980 did not just wreck the country's own tourism industry; it severely damaged tourism to neighbouring Zambia. Tourist arrivals there declined drastically as a result of the withdrawal of ground tour operators, the kidnapping of tourists and hostilities towards them, the use of tourism infrastructure as soft targets for militants, and the restriction of tourist activities as a result of curfews, blackouts and bans on photography. British and US negative travel advisories helped to keep tourists away. Such actions virtually killed tourism in the area.

The Gulf War had a severe effect on tourism in the Middle East, with affected countries suffering a sharp decline in bookings. Direct effects of such wars on tourism include not just fluctuations in tourist traffic but in some cases, the complete destruction of a tourist economy. Ruined economies may result in food shortages, increased levels of crime and threats towards foreigners, such as kidnapping and robbery.

When the Gulf War ended, tourists did not return immediately to the Middle East because they had already found alternative holiday destinations. Even if tourists are persuaded to start returning, the war-affected zone may not be ready to accommodate them again, perhaps not for many years. Wars can wreck whole economies indefinitely.

The negative effects of war on tourism come in many different forms. Demand and supply are not the only issues; the problems associated with war refugees also deserve to be considered. The effects of war on Slovenia's tourism industry following the Yugoslav Wars of the 1990s provide a good example of war's impact on local tourism industries.

Hotel and tour operator behaviour is another important area of consideration in times of crisis. Even an empty hotel will still have to cover many of its short-term costs, so revenue shortfalls represent much larger proportional changes in profits.

Tour operators quite rightly may try to protect their guests by advising them to stay away from areas affected by a conflict. A study of the Croatian War of Independence (1991-1995) demonstrated that in this way a leading tour operator which controls a large market share of the industry can significantly affect the demand of tourists for a particular region. In fact the behaviour of tourism operators in a crisis can have more influence on tourist activity than the messages being sent out by the official organizations.

In 1998, Dr. Sevil Somnez, then at Arizona State University, said: "Tourism and war appear to be polar extremes of cultural activity, the paradigm of international accord at one end and discord at the other... The two practices, however, often intersect: tourism of war, war on tourism, tourism as war, war targeting tourism, tourism under war, war as tourism are but a few of their interesting coupling."

WAR TOURISTS AND 'DARK' TOURISM

There is a long-established tradition of visiting the sites of former battlefields, mass graves and military tombs, particularly those which are of personal significance to the visitor, usually because relatives once fought and died there. The idea of going to see the place where an ancestor died in battle must extend far back into human history, but the facility of modern travel began turning it into an industry after World War I, when groups of British and American people wanted to see the places where this terrible conflict had been fought and where perhaps their relatives had suffered and died. In the

USA, civil war sites like Gettysburg have long attracted those with an interest in their country's history.

War tourism really took off after World War II, and has become a major part of the tourism industry in northern France and Belgium, with peaks in interest at times of key dates such as the 50th anniversary of the Battle of Britain, the Normandy landings and VE Day. The transformation of the memory of war into a sentimental tourism attraction is personified by the memorials of the battlefields of these countries, with their countless thousands of mute gravestones.

War gives special meaning to the places where terrible or noble events once took place. Examples include the sites of battlefields, cemeteries, memorials or monuments and military museums, as well as the harrowing remains of the Nazi prison camps in eastern Germany and Poland, preserved not from commercial motives but so that the rest of us will never forget the atrocities that were committed there. There are now genocide museums in certain parts of the world, including Rwanda and Cambodia, while many tourists visit New York to see the former site of the Twin Towers.

Older conflicts may have less emotional pull for those living today, but remain of great historical interest, particularly to those whose ancestors were involved; examples include the battlefields of the English Civil War and the Scottish rebellions of the 18th century. Ancient battles which today are commemorated by tourism sites date at least far back as the Battle of Crécy (1346); a local museum is largely devoted to the battle.

Although wars which are still ongoing massively disrupt supply and demand and are unlikely to be free from danger, the sites of very recent wars are of great interest to certain types of tourist. One study raises the interesting subject of the 'tourism of war', reporting that some people are attracted to a region by the prospect of witnessing the results or consequences of war

(Sri Lanka provides a good example of this). The terms 'dark tourism', 'black tourism', 'grief tourism' and 'thanatourism' (the tourism of death) have been coined for this relatively new phenomenon. Several studies have shown that war creates a unique form of tourism.

Warfare tourism has become a significant niche market and war-related attractions can thus be considered an important and lucrative subset of tourist sites associated with death and suffering. 'Thanatopsis' is defined as 'travel to a location wholly, or partially, motivated by the desire for actual or symbolic encounters with death, particularly, but not exclusively, violent death'. Whatever we may think about people who feel this urge, the economic benefit of such visits may be important to certain regions. And few people would deny, however atrocious the deeds the Nazis did in their World War II prison camps, that they form an episode in European history which should never be brushed under the carpet.

Tourists have different objectives when visiting the sites of terrible events, depending on their interest in those whose lives were lost - either specific people or entire populations. Visits to private cremations in India or public executions in the Middle East serve as more extreme examples of thanatourism.

Not all the effects of war upon a region are negative. Favourable consequences include the availability of war-related infrastructure such as roads and landing strips. For example, the American military built roads and airports in some areas of Thailand to support its efforts during the Vietnam War. As a consequence, Thailand benefited from the infrastructure that remained after the war had ended. In the Falkland Islands, a new aircraft landing strip built for military use during the Falklands War of 1982 had the unplanned effect of helping to open up the islands for tourism and fishing holidays once the war was over.

COUPS D'ÉTAT

Coups d'état are events in which existing régimes (civilian or military) are suddenly and illegally displaced by the actions of relatively small groups in which members of the military, police or security forces of the state play a key role, either on their own or in conjunction with politicians.

A 1988 study examined political instability in post-colonial Africa by focusing on the effects of *coups d'état* on African tourism development in general, and on Ghana in particular. The national tourism body was challenged by incoming rulers who voided government and its mandates, and the flow of international tourists was curtailed by border closures, thus preventing visitors from entering or leaving a country. There was also damage to the country's image from negative media coverage and travel advisories. A country's development plans may be suspended or cancelled during military intervention.

Travel advisories can cause tremendous damage to the tourism industry of a particular region, as evidenced in The Gambia. For example, in November 1994 the British Foreign and Commonwealth Office (FCO) issued a travel advisory after a bloodless military coup in The Gambia that July:

"Banjul is calm, but the political situation in The Gambia remains uncertain and could deteriorate quickly. Those without compelling reasons to travel should consider postponing their visits. Those with essential business in The Gambia should register their presence with the British High Commission." As a result of this warning, in a matter of days, British tour operators pulled out of the area. Scandinavian operators followed suit shortly afterwards, virtually crippling The Gambia's tourism industry. Arrivals fell from 5,000 to 300, over 2,000 jobs directly and indirectly linked to tourism were lost and eight hotels closed. The country's economic and social conditions quickly deteriorated. This incident confirmed that even bloodless military coups can profoundly affect the tourism of a country through travel advisories.

Coups d'état affect the tourism industry in terms of tourism demand, negative image and decline of tourist confidence towards the safe image of the affected destination. They also affect travellers' perceptions of the political stability and safety of a destination, setting off a domino effect; negative perceptions result in reduced investor confidence in tourism investment among multinational enterprises (MNEs).

In 1997, Dr. Robert Poirier studied the impact of *coups d'état* and terrorism within the context of the changing nature of relationships between MNEs and less developed countries. He confirmed that they lead to the perception of unpredictable events within the political environment, heightening their perceived vulnerability even when they do not cause direct damage to MNE industry interests. Thus, *coups d'état* pose potential risks to foreign tourism investment, and effectively leave the tourism industry vulnerable.

Fiji is regarded as an island paradise, and tourism to the South Pacific haven has increased dramatically since the 1960s. However, a number of *coups d'état* have left it volatile. In December 2006, Commodore Frank Bainimarama, head of the Republic of Fiji Military Force, staged the nation's fourth coup since 1987. There have been a number of studies into the impact of Fiji's multiple *coups d'état* and how the government has since recovered its image. In the year of a coup, expenditure there by Australians was found to fall on average by 65 per cent, New Zealanders by 55 per cent and Americans by 60 per cent. In fact Fiji's tourism industry has yet to recover to its previous levels, and the country's economy has been damaged correspondingly.

Another study confirmed that two periods of political crisis within thirteen years have had a profound impact upon Fiji's tourism industry and its image as a destination. While the recovery programme put in place after the first coup in 1987 was effective, the destination needed much longer periods of recovery following the third coup in 2000. The events of September 11 2001 added an extra layer of complexity, with the island nation among the most vulnerable targets for terrorist attacks. This study demonstrated that an affected destination needs to change its unsafe image in order to regain its old reputation, and this is especially true when that destination has a historical record of political crises.

Another destination which has experienced a considerable number of *coups d'état* is Thailand. Since the fall of the absolute monarchy in 1932, the country has experienced 12 successful *coups d'état* and several unsuccessful ones.

Thailand became a major tourism destination in the period between the 1976 coup and the 1992 coup, with a significant boost in the 1980s caused by the Sri Lanka Civil War, when Thailand benefited because it was seen as the most appropriate alternative destination.

As tourism recovered from both the 1992 coup and the 1997 Asian financial crisis and was expending rapidly, a renewed cycle of political crises began again with the September 2006 coup. Street protests of varying degrees of violence erupted frequently from 2008 through to the May 2014 coup. After the seizure of Bangkok Airport in 2008, the violence in 2010 caused periods of tourism decline, although each time a recovery occurred quickly, with a new record high recorded each year from 2010 to 2013. However, in the aftermath of the six-month long Bangkok protests from November 2013 to the May 2014 coup, tourism did not recover as quickly and by early 2015 it remained well below its 2013 peak. While unrelated factors, most significantly the decline of the Russian rouble and new rules in China limiting budget tours, compounded the effect of the political crises on inbound tourism, the underlying issue remained a loss of confidence in Thailand as a destination. As a consequence, Thailand had to restore its image and traveller's confidence to resolve doubts and revive the ailing tourism industry through vigorous marketing and promotion aimed particularly at high-spending Japanese tourists.

The Thai crises demonstrate that both bloodless and bloody political crises and *coups d'état* damage the tourism industry and the destination's reputation for safety.

POLITICAL PROTESTS, DEMONSTRATIONS AND UPRISINGS

In addition to the political protests associated with the chronic Thai political crisis between 2005 and 2014, recent political crises of this type include the Egyptian protests between 2011 and 2013, the Tunisian Revolution, the Greek street riots in 2010 and the Maldives protests. Such protests and social unrest have hit popular tourist destinations, with tremendous consequences on tourism.

It is important not to underestimate the impact of past political crises, such as those that occurred in Tibet in 1989 during martial law. At that time, tourists who witnessed violent demonstrations and police brutality were urged by local citizens to carry their message abroad. Similarly, the Chinese tourism industry suffered greatly from worldwide coverage of the 1989 Tiananmen Square protests. A 1992 article published in the Journal of Travel Research, by Gartner and Shen, pointed out that occupancy levels in Beijing's hotels had fallen below 30 per cent as 300 tour groups and 11,500 people cancelled travel plans and tourism earnings had declined by USD $430 million.

Mexico's 1994 Chiapas uprising resulted in deaths estimated between 145 and 500 in the first 12 days alone when military troops established road blocks and searched vehicles in the region. Following the assassination of presidential candidate Luis Donaldo Colosio, the situation grew more intense. As a result, Mexico experienced sharp declines in international and domestic tourism, with visitation rates dropping by 70 per cent in January and February compared with the previous year. Chiapas did attract tourists who visited the affected destination following the political crisis, but their numbers did not offset the damage to the image of Mexico among foreign tourists.

Even peaceful demonstrations can severely affect the tourism industry, as evidenced in Thailand with the Bangkok Airport closure in 2008. The Thai political protest grounded on a chronic crisis around the polarization of the main political parties, which erupted into street violence and the occupation of a major international airport which lasted for a week. The closure of the airport profoundly damaged tourism, including hotels, airlines, travel agencies and related industries. It was estimated that the tourism sector could lose upwards of USD $5 billion, a sum equivalent to 1.5 per cent of Thailand's GDP. The most challenging issues faced by the industry were those of international media coverage of the protests and travel advisories issued by the governments of significant tourist generating countries such as the United States, Australia and the United Kingdom.

STRIKES

This type of political crisis may not have as significant an impact as others; but it can seriously damage a country's economy in both the short and long term. Examples of such incidents are the Australian domestic air pilots' strike in 1989 in which an estimated 457,000 people cancelled their holiday plans and a further 556,000 changed them.

A more recent incident was the Qantas industrial disputes. On the 29th of October 2011, the airline's CEO, Alan Joyce, announced the immediate and unprecedented grounding of all Australian domestic and international Qantas flights. Industrial action by unions caused disruptions and delays to Qantas' flight schedule, which cost the airline AUD $68 million. Flights in the air at the time of the announcement continued to their next destination but were then grounded. The lock-out was expected to affect 68,000 to 80,000 passengers on the first day. Some 600 flights were cancelled, with a cost in excess of AUD $20 million per day.

This type of political crisis causes less damage to the tourism industry as the destination image remains unscathed. But these incidents do have significant economic costs for the tourism industry in the long term.

TERRORISM

Terrorist incidents such as the Lockerbie bombing (1988), the Luxor massacre (1998), the attacks of September 11 in 2001, the Bali bombing (2002) and the Mumbai attacks (2008) have been much studied. The difference between crime and terrorism was defined by Dr Valene Smith in 1996 as follows: "Crime is usually one-on-one or an interpersonal interaction; terrorism is a politically motivated small-group activity directed towards individuals to 'strike terror' into their midst and thereby control the opposition. In both instances the activity is local and of short duration. Crime or terrorism leaves little or no heritage to become permanent tourist markers".

In a study in 1983, Linda K. Richter examined the relationship between terrorism and tourism. She suggested that tourists are useful targets for terrorists who seek to disrupt social, political, and economic activity as a means of demonstrating the incapacity of a government to maintain civil order and public safety. This is done with the expectation that the government will negotiate.

Three years later, in 1986, Louis D'Amore and Teresa Anuza assessed the impact of terrorism on international travel, tourists' responses, marketing implications and security issues. They found that the more experienced tourists take terrorism in their stride compared to first-time tourists, who are more apprehensive.

Following terrorist occurrences in Rome in the 1980s, in 1988, J. A. Hurley studied the number of visitors to Rome in 1985 and 1986 and the occupancy rates of major hotels. Findings indicated that American visitors to the eternal city decreased by 59 per cent and occupancy rates went down by 37 per cent for four and five-star hotels. This suggests that hotels which had previously been dependent upon American tourist dollars should shift their marketing emphasis to European and Asian travellers.

In contrast to North American tourists, terrorism was not found to have a significant impact on spending by European travellers. Studies demonstrate that tourists from different countries have different priorities regarding safety and security; some nationalities, including American tourists in particular, may be more vulnerable to problems like terrorism than their European counterparts.

In August 1998, terrorists targeted the US embassies in Kenya and neighbouring Tanzania in nearly simultaneous car bomb attacks that killed 231 people. Following the attacks, several Western countries urged their citizens not to travel to these destinations.

In October 2002, bombings in Bali resulted in over 200 deaths. Consequently, international arrivals as measured by immigration at Bali's Ngurah Rai Airport declined sharply in

2003, operating at roughly 80 per cent less than in the previous year. Both the Kenyan and Balinese terrorist incidents indicated that the governments of the majority of victims' countries tend to react strongly towards the affected destination. An example of this can be seen in the response of the Australian government toward Bali; after 88 Australians were killed there, it discouraged its citizens from travelling to the country.

Terrorism may be attributed to religious fanaticism, political instability, chronic economic problems, famine or disease, environmental problems, demographic issues, lack of opportunities or education, civil unrest, war, guerrilla activity and poverty, among others. Studies confirm that the growth of religious terrorism worldwide appears to account for an increased severity of terrorist attacks.

Brazilian Guilherme Santana said in 2003 that the globalisation process provides the right conditions and environment for terrorism to flourish and become more deadly, as we may all witness from the daily news reports.

CHAPTER 4

THE PROFESSIONAL PERSPECTIVE

This chapter examines the various political crisis situations experienced within the tourism industry.

In the course of the research leading to this book, I interviewed 20 tourism professionals in the UK reflecting the spectrum of tourism stakeholder. Much of this chapter is drawn from these interviews, which added a lot of real-world experience to the academic research and are particularly relevant for this book which is intended to reach past the academic audience.

I have left out some areas of tourism, as they are relatively unaffected by political crises. For example, the Visiting Friends and Relatives (VFR) market is only affected when access to a destination is not possible or exceedingly difficult. One operator explained that because such clients often have in-depth knowledge of the geography and culture of the land, they can usually manage to avoid affected areas of crisis that other tourists may not. Additionally, their strong contact with local friends and relatives keep them updated on situations that arise with a more acute understanding of events than is typically portrayed in the media.

One interviewee who contributed to my study commented that their VFR market suffers no impact from political crises:

For example, in the case of Syria there might be people who will return to Syria... visiting friends and relatives. They are people who have a close connection with that country, for example their family [may be there]. So from our perspective as an organisation, it's an important part of our business because we deal with these groups of people, who when things might be not good from the perspective of a British holidaymaker, of course, the national from that country or someone who has heritage from that country, India, Pakistan, Afghanistan, Iraq, Iran, these kind of countries, where perhaps you might argue that they are unsafe for tourists, but for people who have a connection with that country because their parents or their grandparents come from that country, they will still always go back because they feel they are safer; they have an element of insurance... they know which part of the country to stay away from.

Interviewees commented on the various political crisis incidents they had encountered, including the Lockerbie Bombing (1988); the Luxor Massacre (1997); the Nepalese Royal Massacre (2001); the September 11 attacks (2001); the Bali Bombings (2002); the military coup in Thailand in 2006; the assassination of Benazir Bhutto (2007); the Mumbai attacks (2008); the Bangkok airport closure (2008); the Sri Lankan Civil war (1983-2009); the Bangkok protests (2010); the Manila hostage crisis (2010); the Tunisian Revolution (2010-2011); the Egyptian Revolution (2011-2012); the Libyan Revolution (2011); the Maldives protests (2011-2012); the Jordanian protests (2011-2012); the Syrian civil war (2011-present); and the Kashmir conflict.

Amongst the ongoing crises which affected organisations were the Arab Spring and the past crises in the Asia-Pacific region affecting the tourism industries in India, South Korea, Myanmar, Nepal and the Philippines, and particularly Indonesia and Thailand.

Said one interviewee on the subject:

Unfortunately, tourism seems to be one of the first things affected, whether it's the situation with Iraq and the previous régime causing the war that then follows; and then Afghanistan. All of these things, when there is political unrest or even following on with the Arab spring, with Tunisia, with Egypt, with all of the other countries that are followed, travel and tourism are one of the first things that are affected. People choose no longer to travel to those countries, and obviously Egypt is still feeling the effect of people being cautious about travelling.

Another commented:

We have had political crises, such as very recently in Thailand. The red shirts, the yellow shirts were a massive issue, obviously with the main airport being closed in Bangkok. In fact, we had issues with clients being stuck there, unable to return, and that negatively affected our forward bookings to Thailand and because of the coverage in the news here as well, our Thailand bookings went down. It's been quite recently on Malaysia booking because a lot of people have picked up on the demonstrations in Kuala Lumpur and in Indonesia; also even if the Bali bombings were seven or ten years ago, people are still wary of terrorism particularly in Indonesia, but not so worried about terrorism in Thailand, but obviously that is politically related. It's mainly in Thailand and Indonesia that we come across political issues.

Most interviewees stated that their organisations had recently been affected by the political crises in Thailand and one consultant said his company had faced losing its clients.

All interviewees agreed that when political crisis situations involve violent action and military-related action such as the Egypt uprising, the Thai military coup or terrorist attacks, they tend to have a serious impact in terms of client confidence and the deterioration of the safe image of the affected destination for a relatively longer period. Some interviewees commented on the case of the Bali bombing in 2002, which they claim still affects their organisation ten years on.

An operator echoed these sentiments:

Probably the main one has been the whole Middle East situation we have, but in particular with Egypt, and obviously that started with Tunisia which we don't feature that much. Then Morocco, Egypt, Libya and Syria, where we also had a touring programme. [There were] not many customers, but of course we had to pull all our customers out of the country. But Egypt was the main destination where we had [sic] most customers and where we have to take the biggest action and also where it is still really being felt. I think both in the number of bookings that we had been taking is obviously a lot reduced now compared to what they were previously because people, I think, are still quite concerned about the ongoing unstable situation in the country.

Interviewees also cited experiences of political crises from decades ago, including the Lockerbie Bombing of 1988 and the 1997 Luxor Massacre:

Our company actually lost tourists in that attack and that's probably the most difficult thing in my whole career. The company had 300 people in Egypt at that time.
Specific incidents including military coups, terrorist attacks, demonstrations and protests also affected the perception of Myanmar until about 2012.

On the European front, Greece's political crisis was mentioned by this tour operator:

We've got a similar situation with Greece, primarily because of the economy there with the euro and the street rioting that was causing a few problems. People are less inclined to travel to those areas, and it's also affecting the commercial side of the business because businessmen did not go there either.

Different political situations affect organisations on different timescales. The degree of immediate impact relative to longer-term impact depends upon the type of political crisis. The immediate impact, such as cancellation of tour bookings, occurs when the crisis hits. Then follows the loss of demand after the crisis has passed, due to the deterioration of the destination's safe image.

When a political crisis happens, it immediately damages the tourism industry and its stakeholders, which means hoteliers, airlines, tour operators, travel agents, governments, tourism organisations, tourists and suppliers.

Interviewees in the study reported that the immediate effects of political crises vary according to the main destinations. For example, a tour operator whose main destination is Indonesia was affected enormously by the 2002 bombings in Bali, while one focusing on Thailand had been far more affected by the prolonged Thai political protest:

The bomb in Bali really affected their business. I know a couple of Australian agents... it just crippled their market; they went bust because the Australians weren't going at all to Bali.

Each political incident has particular impacts and repercussions, depending on several factors. The effects can be categorised into two perspectives; the impact on tourism organisations, including perception effects; and the financial effects and the aftermath. These can be influenced or magnified by other effects, which are coinciding effects, ripple effects and spillover effects. The figure on the following page illustrates the effects of political crises along with their coinciding effects. The six effects are depicted under immediate, short-term or long-term impacts.

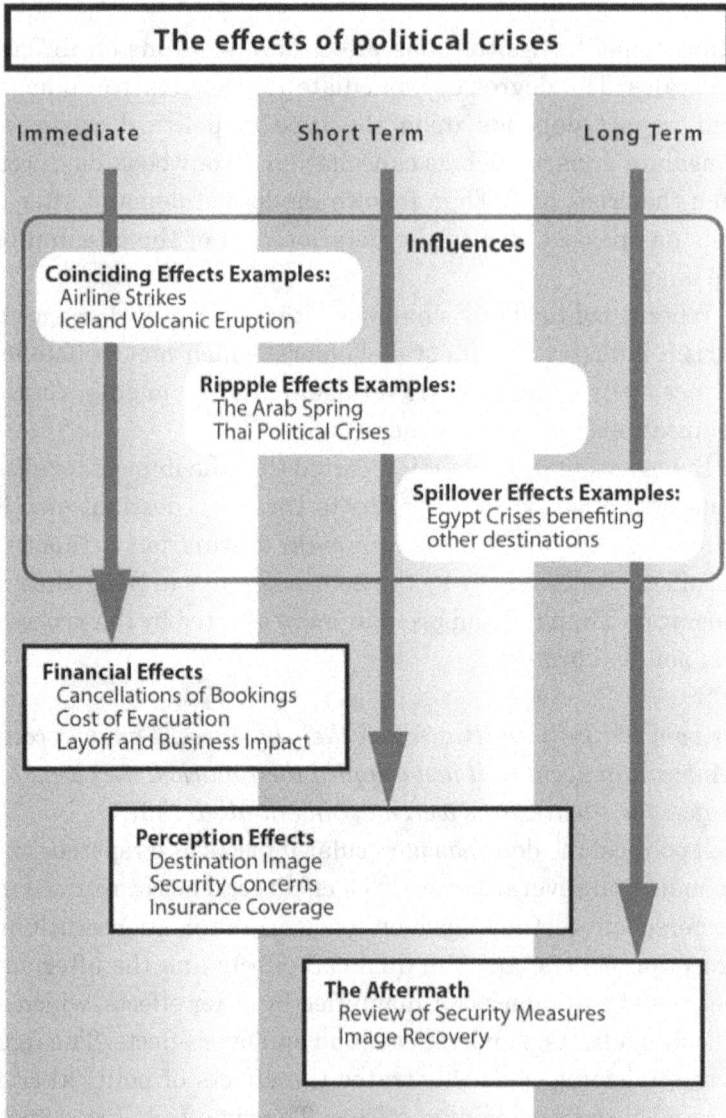

The effects of political crises

Immediate **Short Term** **Long Term**

Influences

Coinciding Effects Examples:
Airline Strikes
Iceland Volcanic Eruption

Rippple Effects Examples:
The Arab Spring
Thai Political Crises

Spillover Effects Examples:
Egypt Crises benefiting
other destinations

Financial Effects
Cancellations of Bookings
Cost of Evacuation
Layoff and Business Impact

Perception Effects
Destination Image
Security Concerns
Insurance Coverage

The Aftermath
Review of Security Measures
Image Recovery

FIGURE 4.1

PERCEPTION AND REALITY

The unsafe image of an affected destination is further sensitized by clients' perceptions. The media play a crucial role in influencing these perceptions by broadcasting reports and footage of political crises which can undermine any belief that the destination is safe or secure, resulting in loss of stakeholder confidence with growing security or fear concerns. Some interviewees agreed that perception effects have a profound impact on their organisations. As their clients lose confidence in the safety of the destination, as a consequence, they lose confidence in their own product, as a travel agent explained:

I think the problem from the clients' point of view is that they see the news and all the news coverage is fires, bullets, blood, people dying, so people look at that and they think they can't get to Thailand.

Half the interviewees commented that the root of a conflict is considered to be a main characteristic. Thus, when a crisis originates from a politically unstable government or an internal conflict between two opposing parties, the situation is regarded as a political crisis. If a government is unstable, it is less likely that the government will be able to control the situation when political conflicts arise. Examples of the results of such conflicts include strikes, riots, demonstrations and protests.

When interviewees were asked about their major concerns regarding political crisis situations, their responses included concerns about military-related situations and those that resulted in negative news broadcasts. The involvement of military force as seen as particularly serious, according to one operator:

A political crisis is something which describes a country whereby the politics becomes unsettled or that might involve the military, with arms being involved, some political groups polling against each other, trying to gain position effectively, trying to wrestle control of the country so it means the army stepping in, or groups with force trying to change the situation, in terms of the reigning power in that country.

Others remarked that negative news regarding political matters increases their concern about a possible crisis:

It's similar to what's happening in Egypt, because Egypt has similar problems to Thailand. Any bad news about political stuff that goes outside the country.

Another way a political crisis can be viewed is the way it is controlled. Most interviewees clearly suggested that a political crisis is, by definition, an uncontrolled event. When such an incident occurs, no trade organisation or other stakeholders (for example, the government, tourists, investors, hoteliers) can control it, leaving it to evolve rapidly into a crisis. An example of this was the Bangkok Airport closure in 2008, discussed earlier.

An operator suggested two additional characteristics that can lead to political crisis situations: the influence of organised crime, such as the Mafia in Italy, and poor management of a destination's government:

It is most of Europe that is in danger: Spain, Greece, Italy, for example. The recent bomb [sic] this year... Sicily; that region is gripped by the Mafia, and in a way we have been going to Sicily for a year, despite the fact that the Mafia operates and controls the tourists. That is very much a political crisis.

When an environmental disaster occurs, such as flooding in Thailand, poor governmental management can also lead to it being regarded as a political crisis, as this operator remarked:

I think the Thailand floods in 2011 were a political problem. The way it was handled... it went off for too long. So many people in Bangkok were helping; the university was being taken over. Flood prevention is a political issue, and things are certainly not perfect in terms of political protest.

Political crises can cause disruption in many other ways, affecting normal life, the tourism industry, and the economy as a whole.

A political crisis can refer to a lot of things; coups, riots, anything that unsettles the situation, unrest or anything like that. London, for example, experienced underground strikes which paralysed the city... so it was really difficult to get around; difficult for sightseeing, late for flights.

Interestingly, some of the interviewees felt that cultural differences affected the identification of political crises. One region may view an incident as a crisis while another does not. A travel agent provided a comparison in this regard between the UK and Thailand:

If you say political crisis, it could mean anything. It could mean internal political crises. Well, we had a political crisis in this country after the election when we didn't know who was going to form the government, but that's a mini political crisis. It's different in Thailand because it could collapse into violence and that is when it affects tourism.

The interviewees' understandings of cultural differences alter their perception of the effects of political crises as well.

Because in the UK, if we think of a military coup, we think thousands of people are getting shot and there is huge military presence on the street. With respect to coups in Thailand, it's very different to a coup in other countries. The military has been part of the Thai culture for many years, and in fact, I think Thailand has had 18 or 19 coups in the last 40 years. Probably the most famous from my perspective was the one in which the King was bringing both sides together. So we know that a military coup in Thailand is not the same.

Cultural differences are a critical factor in the perception of political crises; as one interviewee suggests, such a political crisis would have more impact in Thailand than in the UK. Comparing the impact of past political crises in Thailand and the United Kingdom shows that UK tourists are unlikely to be affected by political crises in their country, whereas in Thailand a political crisis can affect everyone.

On the question of terrorism, most interviewees agreed that it does not constitute a political crisis. A few believe that terrorism is different. While political crises mainly originate within the population of the destination and thus concern local issues, terrorism is considered to be of external origin and may target tourism in order to bargain, negotiate or obtain power from conflicting parties.

Terrorism is a case apart from political crisis. Because political crisis tends to be inwardly focused on the population of the destination and terrorism can be indiscriminate.

The perspectives of interviewees with regard to what is and is not considered a political crisis differ considerably. Whereas one operator did not believe that acts of terrorism qualify, others consider the floods in Thailand and the Mafia situation in Italy to be political crises. Another operator commented that the environmental crises in Thailand can be regarded as political. This demonstrates that many people believe the government of a particular destination is partly to blame, as mismanagement adds to the problems. As the effects of this mismanagement impact the tourism industry, the interviewees perceive it as a political crisis. Thus, regarding terrorism, the interviewees commented that terrorism is also an incident that originates from mismanagement of its government but concerns the international and policy affairs of that country originating more from international conflicts than internal ones.

Understanding how trade organisations interpret the term 'political crisis' is vital to providing a foundation for further analysis. The following sections explore the different effects of various political crisis situations encountered by the interviewees.

If the political crisis involves violent incidents, such as the Manila hostage crisis or the monks' demonstration in Burma, the industry can see short-term issues. With larger-scale incidents such as wars, military coups and terrorist attacks, long-term effects can ensue.

Comparing the effects of Sri Lanka's civil war and strike, the war is a much longer event as it carried on for months or years, which affected the overall selling of tours to Sri Lanka. A strike has a limited time period; the incident took only a few days. In Sri Lanka's case, we make sure we are not selling tours which means sending our clients to those countries.

45

The Libyan Revolution of 2011 affected the image of the entire country. Tour operators therefore stopped selling holidays to Libya even when asked for them.

Probably not after the Libya situation, because it killed the market for people to go back there and until there's stability again, and I think that's going to be a few years for Libya before people start going.

Six interviewees agreed that lack of demand for an affected destination greatly altered their organisations. This factor is a result of perception effects related to the period and degree of political crisis in question:

I think, with the red shirt demonstration in 2010, it started in April and it went on for about 10 weeks, so a lot of business was lost; it was ten weeks of business. It's a long time. Because we have to, you know, it's UK government policy, they have to be sure their citizens will be safe, and so there was so much disruption. Though it wasn't aimed at tourists, you know, it wasn't an easy environment to be in, in Bangkok certainly. It wasn't affecting Bangkok Airport and therefore onwards to other places in Thailand. But definitely, we lost a lot of business... about five per cent.

Some interviewees also drew attention to the impact of loss of insurance cover. Travel insurance contracts frequently contain a clause suspending or withholding cover if government travel advisories recommend against travelling to a destination. Even when it is not banned outright, the difficult of getting insurance has the same effect:

For the red-yellow shirt demonstration, because we had lots of bookings at the time and political crises in Thailand happened, the foreign office sent a message to foreign visitors, especially on the FCO website - do not visit Thailand – so the insurance did not cover any visitors from the UK to Thailand, so we had a lot of bookings cancelled.

Some interviewees agreed that FCO advice is a critical factor when British tourists choose a holiday destination. Moreover, although tour operators are not legally obliged to act according to FCO advice, they tend to follow it and regard it as the most reliable source of information on destinations:

To take the affected destination off sale is not [necessary for] compliance with the FCO; it's more prudent attention to FCO advice. We're not obliged to follow the FCO advice - if we wanted to, we could continue to send customers throughout the entire political situation, but within obviously our duty of care, we take that decision very carefully, because we leave our customers and our shareholders exposed to different kinds of risk, our customers to potential actual harm, our shareholders to legal harm.

It can be concluded from this that the duration of the perception effect is of particular importance. If the perception effect is more long-term, even if it does not involve violence, demand is driven down and tourism companies are forced to absorb the costs on a daily basis.

FINANCIAL EFFECTS

In time of crisis, tourism organisations suffer an immediate financial loss from reduced or cancelled bookings through clients changing their plans and choosing safer destinations. Additional costs, such as those associated with evacuating clients or changing their itineraries, create another financial burden. These effects require close monitoring, as they can seriously erode a business' finances and damage its continuity. As one interviewee stated:

There were enormous impacts on my organisation in terms of our Asia programme. Thailand represents 60 per cent of the business and for four months that business was turned off. It's very hard to say, 'I'm sorry we can't go to Thailand, would you like to go to Malaysia, Bali, or somewhere else?' because they have probably looked through these places already and chosen Thailand because of particular attractions and then it's very, very hard for tour operators to sell a destination that has been affected in sales for quite a long period of time.

In terms of short-term impact, half the interviewees reported that advance bookings had been cancelled due to clients' loss of confidence in the safety and security of the affected destination:

The protests in Bangkok meant people did not go there and people who had booked previously [cancelled]. If they had booked their holiday six months ago, they asked to be sent somewhere else because they were not confident if they would be safe travelling there.

The largest financial impacts come from the evacuation of clients out of the affected area. Inevitably, they wish to return home immediately, incurring heavy costs, particularly where flights are cancelled and different airlines have to be used:

Egypt was disastrous because people didn't want to go via Cairo for their flights. With Bahrain, people were cancelling their flights; they weren't actually connecting flights in Bahrain, people cancelling their flight via Cairo and not stopping in Cairo as well.

ANOTHER OPERATOR CONCURRED:

It was a combination of having customers at the affected destination, how you deal with them, what you do, how you deal with their itinerary, how to manage their worries and fears, and any out of pocket days you might have.

In the case of the 2008 Bangkok Airport closure, many tour operators were obliged to transport their clients to alternative airports in Thailand or Malaysia, incurring further costs:

The yellow shirt demonstration was a massive issue as airports were being closed as a consequence; it affected the clients stuck at the airport, unable to fly in and out.

As tour operators are responsible to their clients until they have arrived back in their home countries safely, they incur the cost of any additional transportation and accommodation that may be necessary in times of crisis:

If people got stuck in Phuket Airport you had to pay for them to go to the hotels. Then, when the customer is due to travel, they are... I would say they're probably the hardest set to deal with actually... the worst financially.

The long-term financial impacts of political crises on tourism organisations are many. They may fail to achieve their annual business goals and objectives, which can be catastrophic. One interviewee, a tourism consultant to many large UK companies for over two decades, suggested that political crises can result in outright business failure, especially for companies that specialise or focus on a particular destination:

Very occasionally, the impacts of political crises can actually lead to the failure of a client due to the fact that they have all of their businesses, or a large majority of them, travelling to a particular destination, and whether the country experiences prolonged political problems; they are not able to diversify quickly enough... they're unable to continue the business.

It is essential for tourism managers to understand the diverse financial effects of various political crisis situations and their effects over time.

THE AFTERMATH OF A POLITICAL CRISIS

The aftermath of a political crisis may bring further complications, for example when governments introduce stricter security, thus hampering tourism. Following the 1997 Luxor massacre the Egyptian government put in place security measures that made it far more difficult for tourists to travel around the country; these measures also altered tourists' satisfaction with their trips, as is evidenced by this interviewee's recollection:

I went to Egypt a few months after the Luxor Massacre. If we went to Abu Simbel from Luxor, Egypt, you still needed to go with the guard and there were only two shifts a day. In the old days we could go anywhere we liked, which means it trims down the opportunity of doing business with the country. Even though this was many years ago, the situation is still like this.

In the aftermath of the September 11 terrorist attacks on the United States, obtaining tourist visas became a challenging experience virtually overnight. This severely impacted the ability of tourism companies to sell American destinations.

The interviewees also spoke of how the aftermath directly affected company policies through altered public policies. This effect tends to be more pronounced in destinations that terrorist attack.

Three effects influence the overall impact of political crises – we may call these coinciding effects, ripple effects and spillover effects.

COINCIDING EFFECTS

The term 'coinciding effect' refers to two or more incidents occurring within the same time frame, resulting in a greater impact. One interviewee explained the combined impact of the Icelandic volcano eruption in April of 2010 and the Bangkok 'red-yellow shirt' protests which followed in May:

At the time of the red shirt riots in May 2010, we didn't have that many clients in Thailand itself because it wasn't high season, but we had a few people who were travelling in the region, [in] Indochina. In their itinerary, their flights included a few days' stopover in Bangkok at the end of the journey. Unfortunately, that period was also compounded by the fact that clouds were over UK airspace. So the two things clashed and it meant that clients who weren't supposed to stay in Bangkok had to stay in Bangkok. Because of the ash clouds, they couldn't get back into the UK, and then all the riots kicked off and we had clients who were staying close to Lumpini Park at Dusit Thani Hotel [in Bangkok] that we had to move.

The coinciding effect is not limited to the tourism industry. One interviewee suggested that the combined impact of the UK economic crisis and the Thai political crisis had an effect on consumer behaviour in general. Booking behaviour had changed; consumers were no longer inclined to purchase a holiday six to twelve months ahead. Instead, because of the economic and political uncertainty, they made purchase decisions within a much smaller window of three months or less:

For the red demonstration in Thailand, I would say it took maybe one year for tourism to go back to the same level for Thailand. There had been so many issues in the year before ... you know, red shirt, yellow shirt, almost on a yearly basis. There was a big focus in the UK news about this because there are so many British tourists in Thailand; there are 900,000 British tourists travelling to Thailand every year.

So the coinciding effects of simultaneous crises can exaggerate people's perceptions. This results in profound financial effects for the tourism industry, on both tourist-generating countries and affected countries.

RIPPLE EFFECTS

Eight of the twenty interviewees commented on the birth of a ripple effect during times of political crisis. Like ripples across the water from a falling stone, the effects of the crisis continue to expand outwards. This often occurs once news of a political crisis spreads to the surrounding region and beyond, even if these regions are not directly affected by each other or the primary crisis. In today's increasingly connected world, ripple effects can detrimentally affect the perceptions of a given area by both tourists and tourism companies alike.

During the Arab Spring, political protests in Tunisia and Egypt affected the sales and safety image of the whole region. Some interviewees agreed that the ripple effect of this event profoundly affected their organisations:

Because my tourists sometimes think Thailand has lots of problems they do not just avoid Thailand. Instead, they might avoid the whole region.

Another interviewee witnessed a ripple effect following the Arab Spring:

Certain airlines have a monopoly on routes; there is no other way of getting to Sharm el Sheikh [than] via Cairo from Europe. I was surprised that even with the problems which were happening inside the city of Cairo, people were not prepared to go via Cairo airport, so that affected us a lot and our diving market for Egypt went down a lot. And also I believe even on long haul, some airlines were affected.

The ripple effect can ultimately serve to reduce the confidence of tourism organisations doing business in a particular region. Such effects magnify the perception of the affected destination, and financial effects follow. In the case of the Arab Spring, tourism companies avoided sending tourists to Middle Eastern countries as the ripple effect swept its way through Tunisia, Egypt, Jordan, Libya and a number of others.

SPILLOVER EFFECTS

The spillover effect presents an opportunity for tourism companies to increase sales of certain tourism products. The China and Japan Island dispute in 2012 had a net positive spillover effect on destinations including South Korea and Australia, as this interviewee recalls:

Recently, there was a political crisis between China and Japan about the islands in the Pacific. In China, there was a lot of anger towards Japan. Japanese cars were kept off the road and Japanese restaurants were boarded up. Thus, the positive spillover was that both Chinese and Japanese tourists went to Korea or even Australia instead.

The above statement addresses both the positive and negative spillover effects on tourism organisations. To reap these rewards, however, it is imperative that tourism managers carefully consider the potential effects of political crises thoroughly, preferably beforehand.

INVESTOR CONFIDENCE

Interviewees agreed that confidence is a key element in assessing whether a destination should be included in their companies' travel catalogues. As the safety of their clients is of paramount concern, they are likely to avoid selling destinations perceived as unsafe, even if these destinations are not subject to FCO travel restrictions.

When asked which strategy they applied to justify the image of safe or unsafe destinations, interviewees responded that their safety perceptions were derived from various sources including the characteristics of the destination, historical political crisis events affecting its tourism industry and how its government has dealt with past political crises.

The first of these factors – the characteristics of the affected destination – includes locality, nationality, culture, infrastructure, and geographical considerations. Thus no two destinations are ever the same. Some boast desirable and safe infrastructure, whereas others do not; attributes such as these can accordingly affect how quickly a destination recovers from a crisis.

The second factor - historical political crisis events affecting an area's tourism industry – refers to the number or frequency of political crises that have shaped the destination in the past. If, for instance, it has a long history of political crises, the perception becomes one of political instability and a lack of safety.

The last factor - how the destination's government has dealt with past crises – is particularly important to consider for tourism's sake. The aftermath of a political crisis depends upon how well an affected destination's government managed, and thus controlled, the effects. If a government has a solid plan in place to mitigate the effects of political crises on tourism, this can reduce or eliminate negative perceptions among tourism stakeholders. There is a heightened potential for trouble in countries with a history of such events, such as Thailand, India and Fiji. It is therefore important to consider how well the tourism industry in this, and other, destinations has recovered from past political crises.

As an example, a tour operator cited her company's perception of the safety of the Philippines for tourists:

We currently don't feature the Philippines in our programme, partly because of the political problems they have had. There was a coachload of tourists from Hong Kong that was hijacked, and also there were some political kidnappings and kidnappings of foreign tourists. So there are many factors why we have held back in selling the Philippines.

Some interviewees explained that they avoid selling certain destinations because of other factors, including perceived ethical issues:

We don't actually operate to Burma (Myanmar). The reason for this is that in my personal view, up until recently the volume of the business that we do would not be proportionate to the negative publicity we'll receive as a tour operator for operating to Burma while Aung San Suu Kyi was in prison or under house arrest. So it was a kind of ethical decision on a personal level rather than a business decision.

However, attitudes towards Myanmar appear to be changing. Both the UK and the US governments have removed their reservation about travel to the country following the release of opposition politician Aung San Suu Kyi from house arrest in 2010. With a new and deliberate policy of welcoming tourists since and restoring relations with other countries, Myanmar's safety image abroad has significantly improved, while tourism has accordingly grown.

Several interviewees suggested that their companies initiated plans to launch Myanmar as a tourism destination following the high profile visits to the country by the then US Secretary of State Hillary Clinton and UK Foreign Secretary William Hague:

I think Myanmar got back-up from the UK government. It's like a reassurance for British tourists that it's okay to visit. I think just recently the foreign minister of the UK visited Myanmar and also the US. Mrs Clinton made it very clear publicly that they are okay, they are open. We are all right. And they don't seem to think election will cause any problems. It's nothing major. It's change for the better, so it's still positive in whatever the outcome.

I think the Myanmar government still has to comply and not do anything horrible.

Thus, as we see, the perception of destinations can derive and evolve from the news and experience emanating from abroad. For smaller tourism operations, confidence remains the key factor. However, for those organisations with hundreds of employees, political risk analysis may also be required before investments are made.

TOURIST CONFIDENCE

Most interviewees stated that they faced the challenge of declining tourist confidence in destinations recently affected by political crises. In the case of Thailand in 2008, the visibility of the violence and chaos on international media outlets led to lost confidence. There was nothing the tourism industry could do other than wait and see how events unfolded, as reflected by the following interviewee statement:

For 2009, basically, we were quite silent for six to eight months because when people are not looking to go to Thailand, [there is] nothing you can do. Whatever you do, they are not going. And that actually affects every tour operator, not just us.

The next section discusses the multitude of information sources relied upon by the interviewees in times of political crises.

SOURCES OF CRISIS INFORMATION

According to the interviewees, major sources of crisis information have been identified as: (1) tourism trade organisations, (2) destination organisations, (3) the media, (4) ground operators, and (5) others, which include travel blogs and local friends.

TOURISM TRADE ORGANISATIONS

Crisis information from tourism trade organisations includes advice from the FCO along with press releases from the Federation of Tour Operators (FTO) and Association of British Travel Agents (ABTA). They each play different roles in providing information to travellers, travel organisation and other stakeholders: FCO advice is the most specific and includes travel warnings for British tourists; information from the FTO and ABTA keep tourists abreast of current crisis situations and travel advice. Most tourism managers interviewed for this study primarily rely on FCO advice. Although this advice does not legally oblige them to take any action, it is nonetheless considered to be the most reliable source of information, and it additionally provides early warnings and risk assessments.

FCO advice can also affect the coverage provided by insurance companies. In turn, organisations seek to mitigate the effects of political crises by dissuading their clients from travelling to a particular destination:

We also take a lot of advice from the Foreign and Commonwealth Office. If they say it's really dangerous to go, then ultimately we have to take that into account because people's insurance companies will not cover them if they travel against the FCO advice.

One interviewee mentioned a multi-resource approach that leverages both the guides of the FCO and information from the FTO. The size of tourism companies influences the way they obtain information and handle situations that arise. One interviewee, for instance, works for a large tour operator with more than 250 employees. She mentioned that she received 'insider news', and was privy to crisis information before the FCO issued its advice. She also commented that she coordinates with the FTO in order to obtain and convey sensitive information in order to mitigate the effects of FCO advice.

Most interviewees in this study follow the advice given by their tourism trade organisations, dependent upon the size of the organisation and its connection with trade organisations.

DESTINATION ORGANISATIONS

Two tour operator interviewees bemoaned the slow response by the local tourism boards of affected destinations in disseminating information in times of crisis. For this reason and others, most tour operator interviewees rely more heavily on ground operators and business partners based at the destinations in question for updates. As this interviewee stated:

During the Thai political protest in 2010, we usually worked with our ground handling people and DMC who sent out the news a lot quicker than the tourism authority of Thailand (TAT). That's very slow. We get the news from TAT a week later.

From interview analysis, it is evident that destination organisations and local tourism board updates are more useful to travel agents, tourism consultants and destination organisations that do not operate tours themselves. Unlike the tour operator sector, which requires real time information to respond to clients, these stakeholders do not. Travel agents, for instance, seek information from their partnered tour operators, who in turn are responsible for locating and assisting tourists affected. Destination organisations' websites serve as a useful source of such information for these tourism stakeholders.

Interestingly, two interviewees who work for destination organisations revealed the importance of conveying crisis information to tourist-generating regions. They stated that destination organisations should collate information from various sources, with an emphasis on accuracy.

THE MEDIA

As has been previously discussed, the media play a critical role during political crises by providing updates to international audiences. However, half the interviewees agreed that the media tend to exaggerate crisis situations, making their information less valuable to their organisations. As one explained this common sentiment:

When the media published some pictures of the flooding in Bangkok, the casual readers or viewers assumed that all Bangkok was flooded. However, the central part of Bangkok was actually fine and most hotels operated normally. Only some of the downtown areas of Bangkok were flooded. For tourist circuits, clients will only have to judge whether it is actually safe or not, so we have to get the information from the ground handlers. We rely more on them than the media and we have to educate clients also that the situation is not as bad as the media may suggest.

Although few interviewees felt that different media sources provide distinct perspectives, a few interviewees said they relied on the television media more than online blogs and websites. The data analysis reveals that tourism consultants tend to utilise this source of information more than other sectors. As interview analysis shows, the media do provide useful means of conveying some information in times of crisis to tourism stakeholders. However, their greatest direct impact is on tourists and potential tourists, as images of political violence and crisis situations can substantially and rapidly degrade their confidence.

GROUND OPERATORS

In this book the term 'ground operator' refers to local business partners, ground handling companies or destination management companies (DMCs), which are located at tourism destinations. According to the data analysis explored earlier, most of the tour operator interviewees derive reliable crisis information from operators on the ground. Because they have staff at the crisis location, they can provide a more accurate and complete picture of events. Long-term relationships between ground operators and other tourism stakeholders can result in effective collaboration during times of crisis, as this interviewee stated:

The destination management company we work with in Thailand is very good at giving pragmatic, sensible, controlled advice about what's impacted, what's not impacted, where [sic] is safe, what's not safe...

One tour operator interviewee noted that during the crisis in Egypt, ground operators in the country effectively coordinated the necessary extra services for her company's clients.

The lack of appointed agents at a particular destination thus leads to greater difficulties for management... making decisions becomes easier when you understand the country and you have a relationship with your agent there and you've been working with them for a while. So something like that can add to the challenges.

In addition, a political crisis in a country like Myanmar, where no such business partners exist, would pose far more problems than a crisis in a nation such as Thailand, which does have established partners. One interviewee referred to this:

Assuming a political crisis is happening in Thailand, it's going to be a lot easier as we have our office there; our people can actually help clients a lot quicker. If it is happening in Burma, that's going to be a lot more difficult. The communication has never been easy anyway. You have to phone them as the internet never works, so basically that's the most you can do – we can't prepare anything for Burma really. We just have to rely heavily on our partner out there.

It is clear that ground operators play a vital role as a source of crisis information for stakeholders in tourist-generating regions. They can give real time information, often with a more nuanced perspective than media outlets. In terms of crisis management, it is imperative to assess crisis situations from multiple perspectives; while the media can play a role in broader coverage, local group operators are far more important in terms of reliable, accurate and multi-sided information.

OTHER SOURCES

Local networks (e.g. friends and relatives), travel blogs and local news provide additional sources of information during times of crisis. Several interviewees said they utilize local online newspapers to establish the views of local people, as well as blogs and discussion forums for further insight. From the data analysis, the firms which rely more on such sources of information tend to be travel agents and smaller-scale tour operators with fewer than 10 employees. They leverage their trustworthy relationships with locals in this way, which can be more efficient than waiting for information to disseminate from elsewhere.

The findings reveal that each sector of the travel business obtains information in times of political crisis slightly differently. The size of the organisation also influences procedures for acquiring information. Travel agents and small tour operators with 10 employees or less tend to use a combination of sources, including ground operators, local news websites and travel blogs. Mid-range tour organisations with 50 employees or less maintain strong contact with their ground operators as a reliable source of information. Finally, tour operators with more than 250 employees obtain crisis information from a combination of sources, including tourism trade organisations, ground operators and their own large networks of employees and contacts in the region.

CHAPTER 5

FORECASTING AND MANAGING RISK

In many cases, seeing a crisis approaching enables authorities and stakeholders to mitigate its effects, either by ensuring arrangements are made to keep tourists safe or by keeping them away from the troubled area, if necessary, until it is safe, thus reducing the risks of tourists being directly affected by violence and disruption.

The most common type of forecasting used in the tourism industry is speculative forecasting, which has been used within the industry since the 1970s. The Delphi approach (based on expertise) is often used for technological and specific events. It was applied, for example, to predicting changes in the Hong Kong hotel industry as a result of the transfer of sovereignty from Britain to China in 1997. The Tourism Forecasting Council adopted a scenario approach based on possible combinations of interest rate rises and currency fluctuations in 1997 when forecasts of inbound tourism to Australia were revised in the light of the Asian financial crisis.

Other types of forecasting are exploratory forecasting, to

extrapolate past trends using regression or time-series analysis based on assumptions about relationships between variables; normative forecasting, to incorporate discussion of the methods needed to attain a desire future outcome; and integrative forecasting, to rely on a variety of methods to determine the underlying relationships amongst a variety of forecasts, integrating these to maximise the forecasts.

In developing forecasting techniques, the tourism sector would do well to draw upon strategic management practices adopted elsewhere.

Forecasting techniques should incorporate recognition of the potential impacts of the underlying political, economic, social and cultural trends that affect each nation as well as the region in which that nation is situated. A study of the case of Indonesia identified deficiencies in current forecasting techniques and suggests that the existing statistical and econometric forecasting techniques are not good enough to deal with the uncertainty of incidents such as the Asian financial crisis, coups in Fiji and the Gulf War.

Analysis of market trends before disasters and crises strike can be undertaken as part of proactive crisis management to provide a reality check on the prospects for particular markets. It is especially important to identify unrelated market factors which may affect a destination on top of the effects of a protracted crisis. Good examples are the degradation of the Russian rouble, which caused a significant decline in arrivals of Russian tourists to Thailand, and the new rules in China prohibiting the sale of zero-cost tours, which caused a significant additional decline in Chinese budget tours into Thailand just at the time of the political crisis of 2013-2014.

For various reasons, markets recover at vastly different rates following disasters and crises, and market-specific strategies and actions need to be formulated based on comprehensive analysis of the precursors and prospects for incremental growth in discrete markets, and possibly even market segments. There is a need to develop new forecasting techniques that incorporate political risk and economic risk and a deeper understanding of the influences of history. A thorough understanding of national history, along with identification of potential risk factors, is essential if potential disruptions arising from these factors are to be incorporated into tourism forecasting models.

It has been suggested that companies planning an investment in foreign country tourism development should consider some form of political risk analysis to assist decision-making.

RISK ASSESSMENT AND PERCEPTION

Risk factors relate both to vulnerability and to the likely frequency and magnitude of hazards in a particular destination. Most risk is either involuntary, which covers most hazards, or voluntary - human-induced hazards such as pollution. Studies show that involuntary risks are better tolerated by the public. Risk assessment is a form of proactive crisis management, in effect.

Disaster reduction programmes should be developed by a range of public and private sectors including government departments (e.g. finance, environment, agriculture, health, education, construction, industry, and social protection and community services) in addition to scientists, non-government organisations and the general public.

As part of their planning, tourists evaluate choices and make decisions regarding attractions, transportation, accommodation and related infrastructure in the places where they are heading. Accordingly, they tend to rely on the information sources they see as most credible, such as government travel advisory information, word of mouth and, to a lesser extent, marketing information. They may consult travel agents and increasingly, surf the internet. If the risk appears too great, they may shorten or cancel a trip or avoid a destination altogether.

Clearly risk assessment should be built into an organisation, its systems and people and become part of a strategic process.

During a crisis, public perception of the affected destination as inherently unsafe is usually conveyed through the news media. In recent years news has tended to break first through the social media, with people using Twitter and other services to alert individuals and groups; news of a major crisis will spread extremely rapidly in this way and reach many people before they have had an opportunity to consult more responsible and authoritative news sources such as official websites and TV or radio news programmes. Studies indicate, incidentally, that women receiving news in this way tend to perceive a higher risk than men do.

Although many incidents affect only small areas, intense global media attention may amplify risk perceptions and lower confidence among visitors, even those travelling to unrelated locations. For this reason it is essential to recognise a crisis early on and deal with issues of perception as quickly and efficiently as practical matters. Competent and well-briefed public relations staff, either employed or retained on an agency basis by the organisation, are essential here. In addition to a plan for handling the physical consequences of a crisis, a well-prepared organisation will have a crisis communications plan in place and ready to be implemented at very short notice. This will involve a clear protocol for who speaks to the media (and who should not), what they should say and to whom, how they deliver messages, and how access to the site for press photographers and film crews is arranged and controlled. After all, it is changes in public perception that cause problems for tourism. "Perception is reality", as one study author has pointed out, and repairing infrastructure will not in itself restore confidence in a destination; the world has to be told about it. Crisis communications will be further addressed in chapter 7.

CULTURAL DIFFERENCES

Tourists' responses can differ according to their nationality. One study on the responses of tourists to Scotland from the USA, France and Germany during two very different crisis situations (the UK foot-and-mouth outbreak and the September 11 attacks) confirms this. French tourists were particularly alarmed by the foot-and-mouth outbreak crisis, while German tourists were more affected by the 9/11 tragedy. One has only to visit Paris or London in summer and see Japanese tourists in their anti-pollution masks to see how important an issue pollution is perceived to be in Japan. This is not because they perceive European cities as being particularly dirty but because they have developed the habit in response to high levels of air pollution in some parts of Japan.

National culture has a strong influence on how people react and respond to crises in global tourism. The phrase 'software of the mind' indicates the deep-seated nature of culture's influence and its unconscious capacity to programme behaviour. The ideas expressed, notably that some cultures accept quite large differentials in the distribution of power, some groups possess a low tolerance for uncertainty and others are status-bound, help to explain the responses of people to stressful situations in global tourism.

Key indicators of altered behaviour after a crisis require further investigation, for example, tourists' propensity for shorter trips, and their turning to car travel following an air crash. Understanding how these characteristics of tourist behaviour may change in the event of a disaster provides insight for tourism marketers, who are then able to create response strategies that identify tourism products designed to satisfy these altered needs.

CHAPTER 6

CRISIS MANAGEMENT

When a crisis occurs, the tourism industry must deal urgently with the immediate issues arising from the event, such as tourist evacuation, stakeholder coordination and media communication. Past events demonstrate that the impacts of crises and disasters can be mitigated or alleviated if action is prompt and efficient. The successful recovery of the Maldives tourism trade after the 2004 Tsunami, as related earlier, is an excellent example.

The growing adoption of formal crisis management is evident from the increasing research on crisis management models and crisis and disaster frameworks for the tourism industry.

THE STAGES OF A CRISIS

Crisis and disaster lifecycles may be broken down in a number of ways to define as many as six stages, but for practical applications we will limit ourselves to the most obvious stages: before, during and after.

STAGE 1 - THE PRE-CRISIS STAGE

This stage varies the most in length; it can range from an extended period to such a short time as to be virtually non-existent. If a crisis is swift to develop, with little or no warning, there may be no pre-crisis stage - such is generally the case with earthquakes and tsunamis. If warning signals are detected only a short time before the disaster strikes, there may not be enough time to deal effectively with the situation (as in the case of the tsunami warning in Japan in 2011). However, even a short warning period will usually allow at least some action to be taken to control the outfall from the event and possibly even prevent it – provided the stakeholders are prepared.

On the other hand, the 2011 Egyptian protests did not spiral into a violent crisis until the protesters had been gathered for a week. But perhaps the ultimate example of a long pre-crisis phase would be given by the Millennium Bug, otherwise known as the Y2K problem. Fears that computer systems and software which had not been designed to cope with the change to a new millennium would malfunction, perhaps spectacularly, as December 31 1999 changed to January 1 2000 led to enormous investment of time and money around the world for years preceding that date. In the event, partly because of the work done to deal with the problem, the Millennium Bug caused only a few minor issues.

From a management perspective, the pre-crisis stage is the opportunity for executives and managers to implement a crisis mitigation plan to reduce risk or put early warning systems in place. An early warning system will allow the threat to be acknowledged and a strategy implemented to mitigate the damage.

STAGE 2 – THE CRISIS ITSELF

The crisis itself, from an initial violent event to resolution, may last a comparatively short or long time depending upon the situation. However, the longer the crisis stage is allowed to extend, the greater the damage to the tourism industry. In the case of the Luxor Massacre in 1997, there was neither a pre-crisis stage nor a stage of intervention. In contrast, wars may present very long crisis stages. During the Sri Lankan Civil War, for example, the long crisis stage allowed time for the region to prepare and implement a strategy to cope with the situation and mitigate some of the negative effects.

Many organisations are reluctant to invest in crisis management planning until there is conclusive evidence of a problem, by which time it may be too late. This is often rooted in the unwillingness of political or industrial leaders to admit to a situation which they know will have disastrous consequences for themselves, once it can be concealed no longer. An extreme example was the pretence to the world's media of the Iraq régime under Saddam that the country was beating back the 2003 US invasion. The Iraqi spokesman Muhammad Saeed al-Sahhaf, who became known to the media as 'Comical Ali', insisted that the Americans were surrendering when in fact there were US tanks within a short distance of where he was standing.

The key to effective crisis management is to do the opposite – to be realistic, to grasp the nettle, to act on the best information available and to prepare for the worst scenario. This means controlling events from as early a moment as possible by being prepared as thoroughly as possible. The former depends on the type of crisis, the latter on the severity or impact of the possible outcome.

STAGE 3 - THE POST-CRISIS STAGE

During the post-crisis phase, image rebuilding and recovery begin and the process of crisis communication becomes critical. This stage may span a considerable period of time. Radical change plays an important role; if a situation remains unresolved, the crisis will continue indefinitely. Thus, effective management of tourism crises depends upon factors such as the availability of reliable contingency plans and funds, the level and type of public and private sector cooperation, and the concerted efforts to change the situation by all tourism stakeholders.

Success in coping with a crisis situation and attracting tourists back to a destination is largely dependent on the post-crisis period. It depends on the level of strategic cooperation between all tourism stakeholders and involves a crisis recovery programme.

CRISIS MANAGEMENT MODELS

Crisis management involves preventing, preparing for, responding to, recovering from and learning from a crisis and its effects. The first use of the term was in a political context: US President J.F. Kennedy used it during the Cuban Missile Crisis of 1962 to describe the handling of a serious, extraordinary situation.

One definition states: "Crisis management involves efforts to prevent crises from occurring; to prepare for a better protection against the impact of a crisis agent; to make for an effective response to an actual crisis; to provide plans and resources for recovery and rehabilitation in the aftermath of a crisis".

In general, crisis management involves three distinct phases as above. The pre-crisis stage includes signal detection, prevention and preparation. The crisis stage encompasses recognition of the event and the initial response. The post-crisis stage may include follow-up information to stakeholders, cooperation with investigations and learning from the crisis event to more effectively manage future events.

Several models and concepts have been developed to help the industry reduce the impacts associated with crises. One divides the process into seven stages, all conveniently beginning with C: cost, contingency planning, culture, control, coupling and complexity, configurations, and lastly communications. The turnaround process includes factors such as organisational learning, reconfiguring the structure of an organisation to respond effectively, creating a responsive and flexible culture and developing managerial competences as part of the management development process. This model has been applied to various studies, including one on the impacts of the September 11 attacks, which conclude that the seven Cs are the most important factors for identifying a crisis and the appropriate response. The turnaround process has been integrated into tourism crisis and disaster frameworks and is among the most important factors in crisis management, as it allows organisations to learn from and improve crisis strategies.

A study of the 1990 flood disaster in Towyn, Wales, introduced a crisis management model which asserted that a crisis occurs in stages. First is the pre-event phase, when action can be taken to prevent or mitigate the effects of a disaster. Evacuations of the population prior to flooding, controlling the number and type of dwellings in the vulnerable area, and the formation of liaison groups to discuss flood problems and possible solutions are all examples of actions during the pre-event phase.

Second is the emergency phase, which may involve a large-scale rescue operation. Here the immediate safety and care of the people affected is the prime consideration of the authorities. The third phase is the intermediate phase, which deals with the short-term needs of people affected by a disaster, such as those in local rescue centres.

After this, management enters the long-term phase, in which the situation progressively returns to normality.

A six-stage model seeking to develop the first tourism-specific disaster management framework was developed in 2001. This was subsequently applied to the Katherine floods in Australia and the 2001 foot and mouth outbreak in the UK.

The success of disaster management can be determined by how well the transition takes place. There exists an acute need for a broader and deeper understanding of this area so that management systems evolve appropriately.

Crisis and disaster management frameworks developed by different scholars have been proven effective in the management of natural disasters; however in human-induced crises such as political crises, disaster frameworks are impractical, particularly during long-term crises such as the Sri Lankan Civil War. A different approach is then required to include actions during the crisis that would normally not take place until later.

PROACTIVE CRISIS MANAGEMENT

The impact of earthquakes, floods, wars, terrorist attacks, diseases and political uprisings has created what many in the media and the tourism industry dub 'a worsening crisis'. Debate is ongoing over what can and should be done to protect tourism stakeholders such as individual carriers, domestic tourists, international tourists, travel-related businesses and their employees from such crises, and how to mitigate their impact on national economies. The purpose of proactive crisis management is to assist the tourism industry in better preparing for crises before they develop.

When an organisation prevents or prepares to deal with crises and their effects, they are engaging in proactive crisis management. Crises may be classified by type, such as an oil crisis or an ecological crisis, while a political crisis may be categorized by internal or external parameters. Some can be prevented, whereas others cannot. Preventable crises typically fall into an internal category, such as those that happen within an organisation itself (e.g. staff illness or staff challenges).

However, it must be noted that the effects of natural crises and certain uncontrollable crises such as those stemming from industrial and political events cannot be prevented by an organisation, though their effects can be mitigated or alleviated. Therefore, understanding the causes of crises that directly affect the tourism industry is mandatory for all stakeholders.

It has been over two decades since organisations were first provided with guidance for preparing for potential crises. Particularly in tourism, there exists a tendency to assume that the unthinkable will simply not happen and thus to ignore preparation. Thus, it is necessary to implement effective preparation and management procedures to determine the difference between industry resilience and vulnerability before a crisis occurs. Destinations lacking an adequate capacity to respond to negative events remain particularly vulnerable and susceptible to crises.

It has been suggested that crisis management concepts such as readiness, response and recovery should be added to strategic management, readiness being somewhat different from response and recovery as it requires awareness, training and tests or exercises. Training reduces errors and shortens the time taken to deal with crisis incidents. Past experience demonstrates that those destinations that employed well-coordinated efforts to regain tourists' trust and increase demand recovered in a relatively short period, as seen in the Maldives in 2005.

The case of Rotorua's tourism industry in New Zealand demonstrates a crisis that evolved as the result of ineffective responses by stakeholders to a changing world environment and a decline in destination quality; two of the main causes were the lack of preparation planning by stakeholders and a lack of forward planning and infrastructure maintenance, which led to a dilapidated cityscape and a magnet of negative media attention.

Tourism organisations must plan for changing environments and unpredictable events. To do so, they must apply critical thinking, in other words thinking the unthinkable. This is the essence of crisis leadership. When crisis leadership is introduced in an organisation, crisis management and communication become a part of the organisation's proactive efforts at eliminating or mitigating crises.

It is essential for all organisations, regardless of size, to have a comprehensive and well-rehearsed crisis management plan while maintaining a continuum of services to meet the industry's response needs in emergency situations. Effective contingency plans and procedures combined with well-trained and motivated personnel serve as the best defence against operational challenges during crises.

POST-CRISIS MANAGEMENT

The post-crisis stage is the period of recovery and assessment after a crisis; this is a point when unique opportunities may be created or additional negative effects may occur. After a crisis has passed, organisations implement various recovery strategies such as marketing, promotional campaigns, public relations and branding, all designed to regain the confidence of stakeholders.

During the post-crisis phase, tourists appear reluctant to return to an affected destination, especially when they find tourism facilities or infrastructure destroyed or damaged; this often leads them to alternative destinations. Some tourists resume travelling following a single crisis event, but investors take longer to return to what they perceive as an unreliable business climate.

Four important considerations should be applied to this phase. First, the long-term impact on distinct stakeholder groups will be different. For example, professional investors have a more rational decision-making system than the casual tourist as they must make a return on their investments. Second, human nature categorises a single crisis event as a 'fluke' where no blame is attached to an individual organisation, yet consecutive crisis events are interpreted as a sign of something more widespread. Third, the perception of risk affects the travel decision-making process; thus tourists may alter their plans, substitute destinations and, in extreme cases, postpone travel. Fourth, it is important to remember that information is conveyed instantly in our digital age; consequently a destination's handling of a crisis occurs in full view of a large and global audience, thus directly affecting public confidence in the recovery of the affected destination.

It has been suggested that mature destinations may recover at a slower rate than destinations in emerging markets. Even so, it is important to appreciate that an affected destination with a chronic history of crises will suffer greater impact as the result of a crisis situation.

The post-crisis period allows organisations to review the impact of a crisis in relation to other recent events. Once the crisis is deemed to be over, it is of paramount importance that continuous efforts are made to recover stakeholder confidence and that the affected destination's government plays a critical role during this phase, as governments can greatly influence tourism recovery through funding major promotional campaigns. National governments can also hasten recovery with tax concessions, grants or loans, while local governments can champion tourism business coalitions that pool together available expertise and resources.

CHAPTER 7

CRISIS COMMUNICATION

Whenever a crisis occurs, the tourism industry must be prepared to manage a flow of information to satisfy the public desire to understand what is happening and what is likely to happen next. Thus, crisis communication is taken into consideration as a means of proactive crisis management so that the tourism industry employs well-planned and well-rehearsed strategies to reduce the impacts of those crises.

In the pre-crisis phase, organisations must develop goodwill with internal and external stakeholders while maintaining reputations. In Turkey, for example, neither the government nor the private sector had in place any plans to deal with the country's 2001 economic crisis, which caused profound effects on the tourism industry that might have been reduced if a mitigation plan had been in place.

In 1995, Michael Bland, in a paper about training managers to handle a crisis, presents six components of crisis management training for organisations which provide a useful framework proactive training, as demonstrated below:

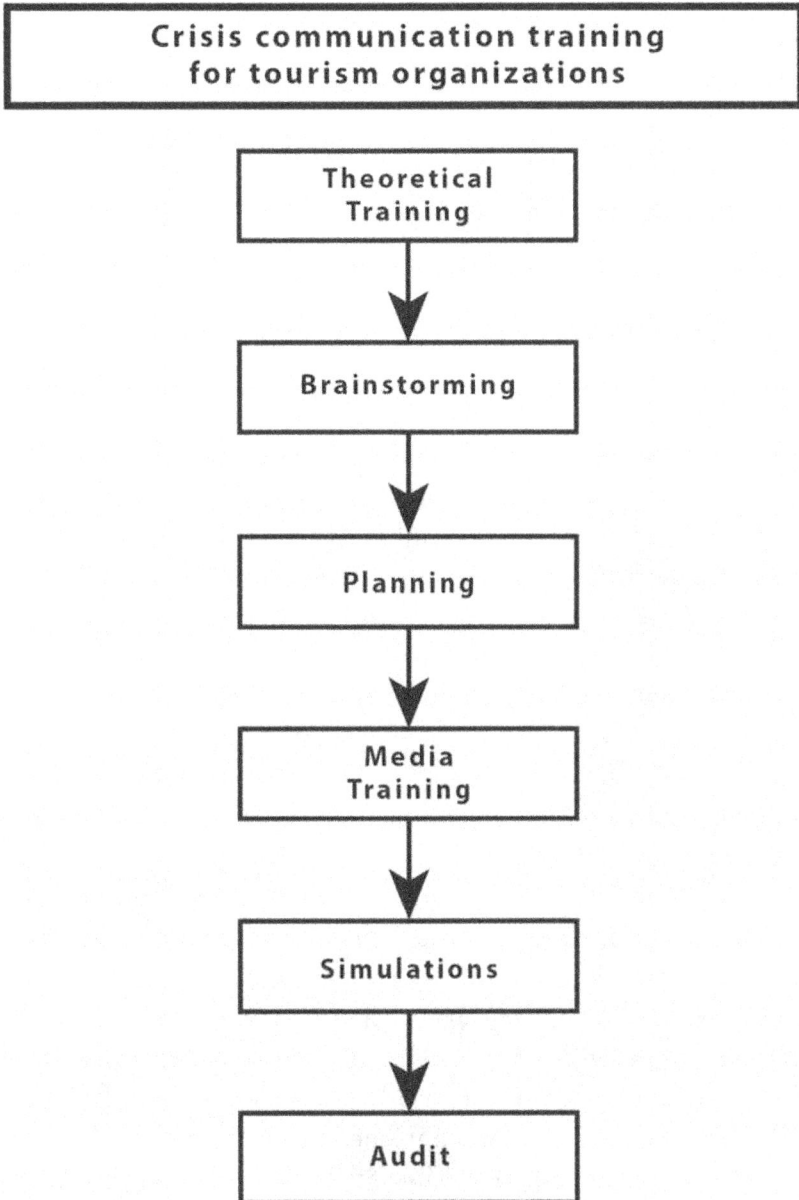

FIGURE 7.1

SECURITY INFORMATION

Security is often an overriding consideration in tourism crisis management, and it needs to be an integral component of crisis communication. Security communication between tourism stakeholders should be acted upon proactively and effectively to mitigate the impact of a crisis. Destinations affected by security situations suffer from a major crisis-management flaw.

STAKEHOLDER COORDINATION

Tourism literature divides crisis response into two main categories, internal and external. Internal response refers to stages where management assess conditions internally; this involves reassuring guests and staff, determining additional dangers, mobilising emergency preparedness, protecting the safety of people and property and establishing information outposts. After the internal conditions have been established, management then coordinates externally with the local community. These actions should be implemented through pre-established, efficient channels. It is clear that crisis response requires coordination between tourism stakeholders, both internally and externally.

Having said that, it is vital that external communication is not delayed until the organisation feels it is ready; 'ready' for the organisation may be far too late for the outside world. Some news will leak out almost immediately, so the flow of information must be controlled from the outset. In practice those responsible for communication will need to work in parallel with those managing the situation inside, not in arrears.

The stakeholder response itself will affect the overall impact of a crisis. A study of tourism responses to the 2001 foot-and-mouth outbreak in the UK confirmed that the impact was affected by stakeholders' responses and how they were portrayed in the media. Key stakeholders included the government and trade organisations. The lack of effective coordination and communication led both to the failure of the government to recognise the real problem and its initial apathy in grasping the potency of the media despite conflicting reports. Crises can worsen if there is a lack of stakeholder coordination.

CRISIS COMMUNICATION RESPONSE

Past research on tourism crises highlights the need for crisis management frameworks which include effective communication strategies directed towards potential tourists and the mass media. Crises create uncertainty for stakeholders, so minimising this uncertainty through the provision of information is paramount. In a crisis, people tend to depend on the media more than usual.

Failure to respond allows the media to take control of public perception by defining the situation. When the crisis occurs, crisis communication response strategies already in place should be implemented; it is too late to create them. This ensures that the destination's image experiences as little negative publicity as possible. Timely and accurate dispersion of that information is vital, as is the deployment of adequate resources to counter the impact of a crisis by organisations; the methods of putting those communications to use appropriately; and finally, the use of a single authority, a press spokesperson or a small designated team, to handle media enquiries.

Policymakers are challenged on the content of messages that should be communicated. Research in crisis communications focuses on two distinct areas: form, such as how the crisis response is presented, and content, such as the actual messaging used in the response.

The three key informational needs are to supply background information on the crisis event, to explain how those involved will be affected and to detail what precautionary measures those affected need to take. Blame and responsibility are considered crucial issues for those affected during a crisis or disaster.

Events are influenced by a number of factors, and this is where crisis communication response strategies particularly play out, as there may be opportunities for decision-makers to handle a crisis. The 2004 Madrid bombings and the 2005 London bombings serve as a good example. The British Government displayed highly effective communication by responding early to concerns of a possible link to Islamic extremists and defining the bombings as actions in direct opposition to the British way of life and the London spirit, which necessarily included all people, including Muslims. Conversely, the Spanish government failed to effectively define its problem, which resulted in difficulties in conveying judgments regarding those involved in the events and endorsing remedies for the situation.

POST-CRISIS COMMUNICATION

A good communication plan can lead to rapid dissipation of negative images and a quicker recovery. The cost of preparing a crisis communication plan in tandem with a marketing recovery plan is likely to be small compared to the impact on decreased visitor activity and flagging consumer confidence of a slow response to a crisis or disaster.

During the post-crisis phase, organisations focus their efforts on reputation management and returning the organisation to a sense of normality. It is difficult for trade organisations to compete effectively with the mass media, which have worldwide 24-hour coverage. On the other hand, social media offer effective communication channels which can offset and often influence mass media reporting by publicising the positives and reporting the progress of the recovery in real time, and destinations can seize some control to restore confidence. It is important for the tourism industry to learn as much as possible about what could deter the market segments it caters for; methods of information delivery should be investigated to ease the concerns of travellers. For example, a military conflict may be confined to a particular region of a country while other areas are left unaffected.

Positioning and repositioning strategies are suggested for the post-crisis phase. A repositioning strategy is an approach to positioning which seeks to manipulate what already exists in the mind. For example, in the case of Fiji, its peaceful island retreat image was damaged; a repositioning strategy improved the situation. Likewise, Montenegro repositioned itself in its post-civil war climate as a destination for sustainable tourism. By reinforcing its role as an environmental leader in the Mediterranean, the small Balkan country can further distinguish itself from similar destinations.

Regarding the case of New Orleans following Hurricane Katrina in 2005, in which more than 1800 people died and property damaged topped $100 billion, one study has suggested that recovery marketing strategies can be more effective if the repositioning work undertaken by tourism marketing organisations is included. It also suggests the inclusion of the lessons learned for post-disaster market repositioning.

In "Marketing for hospitality and tourism" in 2005, Kotler, Bowen and Makens defined market position in a communications strategy as "the way a product is defined by consumers on important attributes – the place the product occupies in consumers' minds relative to competing products". A successful positioning strategy works by reinforcing positive images already held by the target audience, correcting a negative image or even creating a new one. Positioning can be done by product attributes, price, competition, product class, user, and/or application. While positioning strategies may be carefully planned and orchestrated, the major problem during a catastrophic event is that the mass media coverage of the disaster can overwhelm other messages about a destination's market position.

Events that occur in remote locations or with less media visibility have much less effect than those in well-known destinations or those significantly affecting tourists. The Somali Islamist attack on the luxury beach resort of Kiwayu, Kenya, in 2011 mentioned earlier is such an example. As noted above, the impacts of disasters on the market are often out of proportion to their actual effects on the ground, because of exaggeration by the media.

So post-crisis communication must be examined in relation to how the perception of the affected destination has been communicated. This means that how well organisations can manage perceptions becomes a key issue. Crisis recovery strategies aim to achieve two fundamental lines of action: the first is action over reality, and the second is action over the mental image or the perception of the reality. These can also be approached as strategies to decrease respectively real risk and risk perception.

CHAPTER 8

PICKING UP THE PIECES

RECOVERY MARKETING

The task of rebuilding the tourism industry in a city or country hit by a major crisis may be enormous, amounting to many millions of dollars and taking many years. If the crisis is a major one, it may never be possible to restore the resort's image to the way it stood before the event, but that does not mean a thriving tourism trade cannot be recreated, given the right strategy.

Marketing recovery strategies need to be adapted to match the more significant issues specific to each recovering destination. Some may be centered on pricing or innovative packaging, while other situations may be best handled with a media campaign to reach potential visitors directly. An integral part of effective marketing management of crises is for tourist authorities to establish and maintain alliances with trade organisation and government stakeholders that share common vested interests (e.g. airlines, hotels, resorts, museums, attractions and wholesale tour operators).

Recovery marketing should aim to convince potential visitors that they will continue to experience the features which draw them to the destination, perhaps rest and relaxation or a healthy natural environment, despite the recent crisis. Other strategies include the rapid renewal and repair of tourist facilities and infrastructure as well as the accurate but rapid delivery of information through key visitor information sources. Identifying and leveraging opinion leaders with the dissemination of positive attributes of a destination can further offset negative publicity emanating from the mass media; effective advertising campaigns capitalise on visitors' nostalgia and mental connections to the place, as was demonstrated in the case of New Orleans after hurricane Katrina.

Price discounts, commonly applied to attract potential visitors during the post-crisis phase, have been widely used, although there is a risk of devaluing the already damaged image of the recovering destination; indeed price cuts may be seen as confirmation by the industry of the reduced value and desirability of the destination. The main thrust of recovery marketing strategies is not to discount but to prevent cancellation in the short term, so that existing bookings are honoured and sales are maintained.

Recovery marketing strategies should be implemented in the short, medium and long term, where the short-term function is to stop cancellation and use both traditional media and social media to correct the misapprehension that the destination is in danger, as after the tsunami disaster in the Maldives in 2004. While the loss of life was far smaller than that of other destinations affected, the damage to the infrastructure was devastating throughout the entire destination and the images propagated through the global media showing the worst damage were bound to trigger mass cancellations. Yet the prompt and effective recovery strategies that were devised and put into action immediately after the disaster allowed the Maldives first to salvage many of their upcoming bookings and quickly rehabilitate the resorts least damaged, and second to create marketing campaigns specifically designed to attract new tourists, in this instance surfers, in the low season. A similarly successful long-term strategy was also implemented for 2007 and beyond, allowing the Maldives to recover far sooner than other affected destinations in the region.

Almost immediately after the November 2013 typhoon Yolanda, the Philippines tourism board reacted quickly with aggressive campaigns. By coincidence, they had just begun a campaign in the UK a few weeks earlier to promote the first direct flight to Manila in over a decade, which enabled a quick and effective short term response.

Diversification of the affected destination's products and market can help in post-disaster marketing. This is especially true of iconic cities and regions which can retain their position among the world's leading destinations, as in the case of London. Emergency actions can affect the marketing of a destination during the post-emergency stage, thus emphasising the need for long-term, sustainable stakeholder partnerships for the destination to prosper.

A study of a shift of Canadian seasonality and domestic travel patterns following the September 2001 events has suggested that it is imperative to develop crisis recovery marketing policies such as preparing emergency marketing plans that focus on altering traditional markets for safer ones. An effective marketing plan is needed to communicate the outcomes of policy changes to the consumer. There is a need for ongoing research into how travel markets react to different disasters, such as tracking tourist behaviour and travel patterns while indicating dislocations and trends.

A recovery marketing strategy can be designed by including the tasks below:

- Gather all the elements to lead to a coordinated response.

- Identify the primary messages.

- Be proactive: reach the media and feed them constructive news.

- Maintain a sustained and visible presence in social media.

- Survey and analyse generating markets anew, don't assume anything.

- Restore brand confidence.

- Increase visibility through partnerships past the travel industry.

- Offer incentives and promotions.

- Increase familiarization trips for the media.

- Seek social media personalities to include in familiarization trips.

- Track and review all your marketing activities frequently to adapt quickly.

A study of the impact of Cyclone Larry on the North Queensland tourism industry looked at the issue by examining the impact on visitor flows in the short term and recording the views of visitors who travelled to the region several months after the event. This cyclone, which struck in March 2006, caused more than a billion dollars' worth of damage to the state. Results suggested that once essential services were restored and the affected area was safe, marketing played a major role in informing visitors that the area was again 'open for business'. However, a study of the Hong Kong outbound tourism market in the immediate post-SARS period suggests that markets rebound quickly once the immediate crisis abates, possibly suggesting that the magnitude of the rebound is in direct proportion to the extent of privation felt by affected individuals.

An organisation cannot provide a quality service to the public without the implementation of a well-orchestrated public relations programme. The tourism industry has shifted towards increased use of PR tactics to communicate messages to key stakeholders; accordingly, tourism managers utilise a growing number of public relations information channels when communicating with their target audiences. Frequent use of print media PR reinforces how managers continue to disseminate messages via 'uncontrolled' methods. These outlets, though often viewed with more credibility because of their filtering via gatekeepers such as editors and producers, limit the organisation's control over the published content, style, placement and timing of the message. Despite these shortcomings, receivers of this information may perceive PR as more genuine and absolute.

Having discussed various marketing strategies for the post-crisis phase, it is clear that marketing recovery strategies play a crucial role and often dictate how soon affected destinations recover from a crisis.

DESTINATION IMAGE

The successful development of tourist destinations depends on the perceived image that tourists and residents have of the present and future situation of a destination. As a result of media coverage and social media influence, perceived risk associated with a particular destination may be far greater than the reality on the ground.

Destination image has been said to consist primarily of two components, cognitive and affective. This emphasises the importance of destination 'personality', which deserves consideration alongside a destination's image. Brand personality may be described as the traits associated with humans that consumers perceive brands to possess, such as friendliness and openness. A distinctive brand personality can create unique and favourable associations in the consumer's mind, thus enhancing the value of the brand even if the destination is hit by a crisis. Like brand personality research, the academic literature increasingly acknowledges the importance of destination personality; in particular, the importance of leveraging the perceived image of a place and influencing tourist choice by improving a destination's image in the recovery phase.

The images cities have can affect a multitude of decisions by the public including those concerning tourism, migration, investment and businesses. Image also affects decisions by policy makers regarding revenue grants, capital and resource allocation, legislation and rule-making. Finally, the perceived image of a destination affects the self-image of its own inhabitants.

Until recently, information about a geographically distant location was not on the radar of most people, so they made no attempt to verify the situation. Media reports from distant lands were viewed, generally, as bona fide and objective. But the increased acceptance of information conveyed through social media has substituted the distance factor with that of the degree of personal connection the recipient has with that of the sender. A report, however casual and limited, from a personal acquaintance or even a casual social network 'friend' has more weight in the recipient's mind than any traditional media, possibly even more so for a distant location. Thus, even a steady flow of accurate information between local agencies and the media is no longer sufficient to overcome the crisis's negative repercussion damaging the destination. Active engagement in social media is now equally critical to the success of the strategy.

The figure below shows a model of the factors leading to the creation of images of the political instability of a destination. This model includes elements first identified in 1996 by C. Michael Hall and Vanessa O'Sullivan.

However, the mass media have an influential role in shaping the image and perception of destinations in times of crisis.

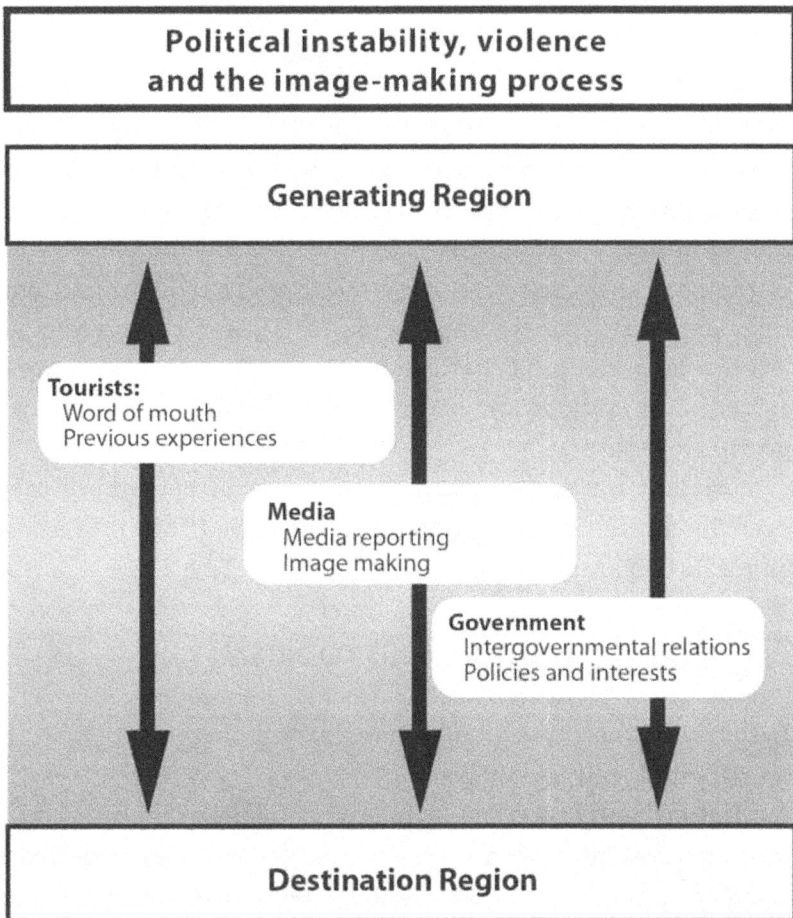

FIGURE 8.1

Thailand serves as a good example of this effect. As a result of the political conflict in Bangkok in 2010 and the ensuing travel advice from tourist generating countries, the number of tourists fell by 20 per cent. These crises of perception can bring about more destructive mayhem than the damage created by the political crisis itself.

Conversely, good management of a crisis can actually improve the image of a destination. Heroes are born, change is accelerated, latent problems are faced, early-warning systems develop and new competitive advantages appear.

Sometimes of course destinations fail to learn from their errors, insisting that continuing the same policy is all that is required. In "Organizational learning II: Theory, method and practice" in 1996, Chris Argyris and Donald A. Schön explained that 'single loop learning' occurs when the values and norms underpinning a strategy or action are left unchallenged and unchanged, thus preventing organisations from learning from their errors; this potentially leads to failure. The answer is 'double loop learning', which promotes inquiry, challenges current assumptions and actions and leads to new theories to provide foresight.

Previous tourism literature also confirms that there is a need for destination marketing organisations (DMOs) to focus on resolution and feedback.

POLITICS AND TOURISM

Historically, there has been little research and literature linking tourism and political sciences.

As tourism plays a major role in influencing international relations, in the international arena (where most relations between nations have a political component) it is inevitable that tourism development will have strong political implications. In

1983 Linda K. Richter noted, in "Tourism politics and political science: a case of not so benign neglect", that most nations base their policies toward foreign tourists on both the anticipated length of stay and the degree of international cooperation existing between the two countries. For example, the United Kingdom requires no visa from citizens of Malaysia, but it does require visas from citizens of other countries in the neighbouring region including Thailand, Indonesia, and Vietnam. Thailand similarly shows its motivations to promote tourism by waiving visa application fees for citizens of South Korea, Peru and Brazil. Reciprocating, South Korea, Peru and Brazil likewise do not require visas from visiting citizens of Thailand.

The visa factor is one of the fundamental mechanics used to boost tourism to a particular country. Korea, for instance, is still the major outbound destination market for Thai tourists, due to the short distance between the two countries, the availability of low-cost airlines and the absence of visa requirements. Government leaders accordingly perceive tourism as a political bridge between nations. Another important consideration is that tourism politics have been largely overlooked by political science, even though relations between individual countries by means of multinational corporations such as hotel chains, airlines, tour companies, and credit facilities are of tremendous political importance; many have more financial assets than any other industry in their respective countries. The ramifications of this extend to financing, managing and controlling the tourism industry in such countries.

From the public administration perspective, the efficiency of public services has a significant effect on tourism. This can be crucial to those destinations which are regularly affected by political crises. Public administration likewise plays a major role in the recovery period of a crisis. In normal circumstances, aspects such as crime levels, friendliness of residents, safe roads and aesthetics are examples that illustrate how well-monitored public administrated tourism development can influence tourist satisfaction.

GOVERNMENT CONTROL OF TOURISM

By manipulating visas, currency regulations, internal access and export and import procedures, public policy directly affects tourism and controls the numbers of tourists as well as their spending. The OECD (2006) advocates a whole government approach to tourism policy, moving beyond tourism-specific policies towards recognising tourism as a sector that includes a wide range of activities across economic sectors. This involves horizontal and vertical linkage at the national and regional levels, therefore involving many government departments.

CHAPTER 9

APPLYING POLITICAL CRISIS STRATEGIES IN THE TOURISM INDUSTRY

Having discussed the key effects of political crises, what about the crisis strategies implemented by the industry? This chapter addresses crisis mitigation, preparedness and response and recovery strategies, and identifies the most influential factors that render a destination more resilient to the effects of political crises.

CRISIS MITIGATION

These strategies are applied by trade organisations to mitigate the effects of political crises on tourism destinations. They include methods of risk reduction, perception assessment and travel insurance.

RISK REDUCTION

Every stakeholder interviewed suggested ways of reducing the effects of political crises. They included leveraging connections with local citizens and business partners in addition to the media to pinpoint potential liabilities, recognizing risks to identify the potential impact on the tour operations on the ground and taking steps to mitigate those risks, which may include limiting or withholding sales to that destination.

Tour operators involved in Indonesia described the risks associated with operating tours following the 2002 Bali bombings; it took a full decade after the incident for their organisations to reconsider the destination, only after the risks were deemed acceptable. This comment reflects their caution:

Only now we are re-launching Indonesia again because ever since the bombing, there has been a lot of tension, [fear of potential] terrorist plans to attack places frequented by tourists.

Like Indonesia, the Philippines is a destination that continues to be regarded as unsafe due to conflict between minorities. Some operators mentioned that they eliminated liability altogether by not sending tourists there. The Philippines has been excluded from one of these operator's products for the past ten years because of these concerns:

We currently don't feature Philippines in our programme partly because of the political problems they have had, but I think in terms of what the FCO are advising they are opening more and more. The country is becoming safer in the capital and around the northern islands of the country, so if we were to reintroduce the Philippines, we would put strict limitations on where our clients can go, because I believe there are certain areas that are still not safe.

Similarly, two interviewees stated that their respective companies applied risk reduction strategies in Thailand by not selling tours in areas of conflict (namely the three southern provinces of Pattani, Yala and Narathiwat). Although these organisations sell packages to other parts of Thailand, they only do so with proper crisis plans in place. If problems in the three southern provinces were to escalate and spread to tourist areas like Phuket or Bangkok, they would be prepared to manage the potential effects:

It's very, very difficult to plan because every situation is different. There are different consequences to very different situations; I mean the ongoing problems in southern Thailand - in Yala - never affected tourists but that could move to Bangkok and, realistically, it might well happen that bomb blasts go off in Bangkok. We kind of recognise that but it's never happened so far.

About half of the interviewees articulated how they apply risk reduction strategy by foreseeing potential risks of political crises at each destination; they then design their tour itineraries to exclude areas where either uncertainty or a history of political crises exist. A few interviewees concluded that some destinations and their associated risks are more expensive than others. For example, the cost of risk in selling Thailand-based products is far higher than in the case of Vietnam, as the latter country poses a lower risk of political crisis. As a consequence, these interviewees opted to promote Vietnam as a destination instead of Thailand.

PERCEPTION ASSESSMENT

Interviewees also talked about their experiences in the time leading up to political crises; they agreed with one another that bad news such as movement in the opposing parties, ongoing conflicts or amendment of government policies generally precede crisis events. They added that they utilize these indications to implement effective courses of action in advance. One interviewee, for instance, commented that when a political crisis materialises organisations should be ready for all possible effects. They need to know the number of customers affected, the available airlines serving the area or other transportation alternatives, and such details as contact information of clients and their relatives.

Additionally, half the interviewees suggested that it is essential to evaluate the situation once news has been obtained so as not to ignore potential problems or make quick assumptions. For example, in the case of the 2010 elections in Myanmar, this tour operator confirmed that they waited for the outcome and the direction of the newly-elected government before deciding whether to include the country in their travel products:

With the Burma programme, there isn't really advice by the Foreign and Commonwealth Office against travel to Burma (Myanmar). It is a political reason that held us back from selling Burma. However, in 2009 we had information that led us to believe that this was changing; hence I started doing research on launching holidays [and] group tours to Burma. At that point, because Aung San Suu Kyi was still under house arrest, we had to make sure that what we offered to clients was safe. It wasn't government owned, so there were lots of terms and conditions that we had to stipulate in order for us to sell Burma.

Once official news had been reported, a few operators assessed the situation further by obtaining additional information from their contacts on the ground, such as local ground operators and business partners:

It's very difficult to plan ahead because every political issue has a different resolution, you know. We can follow the politics in Thailand, but ultimately if we speak to Thai friends, it's like okay what's happening out there; elections are coming up out there; potential problems; demonstrations; it's very difficult, you know, for anyone to say for sure, you know, we have to ask what possible risks are out there in the next year

In summary, most interviewees implement perception assessment of tourism destinations to plan in advance for crisis events. Excluded from these assessments, however, are most terrorist attacks, which by their very nature, generally cannot be predicted.

INSURANCE COVER

Travel insurance plays an important role during political crises. Although such insurance cannot alleviate all the issues facing a tourism organisation following a crisis, it can help them to reduce some or all of the negative financial consequences. Companies issuing travel insurance pay for most costs incurred by their policy-holding customers who find themselves affected, although depending upon the extend of coverage purchased, these costs may include rescheduled flights, extended accommodation nights and hospital visits related directly to the crisis (such as victims of violence):

To prepare, generally when clients book with us and they put down the deposit we confirm all the arrangements. We always try to make sure that they have travel insurance because it can protect them if they need to re-route their holiday.

Thus, travel insurance can be used to cover the risks of tourism operations, thereby guarding organisations against costly events that otherwise may have a crippling effect on their business.

It should be noted that travel agents have a strong incentive to sell travel insurance to their customers, as the commissions earned contribute to their sales margin.

The discussion of crisis mitigation strategies applied by all of the interviewees reveals that it is still possible for organisations to lessen the impact of political crises, thus becoming less vulnerable. This is done by integrating a crisis mitigation strategy into a comprehensive crisis management plan for all key positions within an organisation.

CRISIS PREPAREDNESS

A number of stakeholders apply largely similar crisis preparedness strategies. Although two interviewees noted, interestingly, that there was no effective way to pro-actively prepare for future crises, the vast majority of companies do have three main crisis preparedness strategies in place: (1) diversification of tourism products, (2) strengthening communication at times of crisis, and (3) market segmentation.

DIVERSIFICATION OF TOURISM PRODUCTS

At least some, if not all, stakeholders apply diversification strategies in order to prepare for the effects of political crises. Regarding diversification strategy, some companies can diversify the risk of the products in their portfolio as they do not depend solely on sales of one product or destination, so they can still offer alternative products, should a crisis occur in one location; they can likewise easily divert customers to other destinations rather than lose all their business. Particularly in areas or circumstances where a destination is more likely to suffer a political crisis, most organisations have lists of alternative destinations. Thus if one area is affected by a crisis, the organisation can offer the client an alternative that remains unaffected.

Several interviewees pointed out that it was not smart to consolidate destinations, thereby 'putting all their eggs in one basket'. For companies who focus on a particular destination, political crises can have a profound and very serious impact as stated by this tour operator:

Because we specialise in Thailand and focus only on this destination, once the political crisis happened in 2010 all customers cancelled their tours and looked at other tour operators to go elsewhere. We learnt not to put all our eggs in one basket. After the Thai political incidents, we expanded our products to more destinations by not working with only one destination.

By contrast, one operator specialises in gastronomic tours and thus is not as seriously affected by political crises. His company sells food experiences and is not focused on any particular destination. In cases of crisis, unaffected destinations can easily be substituted. Yet a diversification strategy itself involves risk and costly expenditures that ultimately cannot guarantee an organisation's success:

Unfortunately, more often than not [adding destinations] results in a lot of expense in trying to set up a brochure, marketing, and getting contracts in place... they don't have the same advantages, the same knowledge, and the same context as they do in their primary destination.

Diversification is one of the most effective crisis preparedness strategies in alleviating the potential risk of political crises, particularly at destinations more likely to be affected by political conflict.

STRENGTHENING COMMUNICATION

Faster communication is crucial when preparing for potential crisis events. Specifically, communication with other stakeholders within the industry is of utmost importance. Therefore, it is incumbent upon an organisation to strengthen communication platforms before political crises arise so that decisions can be made faster and more accurately in times of crisis as pointed by one operator:

It is important to strengthen communication to prepare for times of political crisis through developing relationships with different stakeholders within the tourism industry; [to] be more pro-active, especially with our ground operators who are located at different countries and different airlines. Because during times of crisis, you really need strong communication lines with people within the industry to assess crisis situations in order to make fast and accurate decisions.

Effective communication needs to be established in advance to deal with the effects of political crises. When a crisis occurs, information is conveyed to tourists and hotel suppliers at the affected destination so that they can negotiate cancellations, airline partners who transport clients away from the affected destination and ground operators who organise the logistics. As another interviewee stated:

The most important in the whole crisis management procedure is communication with the clients and the local ground handlers to update us with what is going on. Sometimes they may know what is happening, whilst the outside world can only watch the news. That is the most important thing - clients' safety- by communicating.

Communication strategy can be strengthened in two ways: internal crisis communication and external crisis communication. Both areas require cultivation in order to strengthen an organisation's patterns of communication before a crisis hits.

A number of interviewees commented that internal crisis communication is one of the key issues taken into consideration. To lessen the effects of crisis and take the proper action at the right time, management decisions must be effectively communicated within an organisation. Some also spoke to this awareness, commenting that should a political crisis occur, they would immediately know what actions to implement in order to best facilitate the handling of their customers in the affected countries. Clearly, their respective organisations have strengthened their ability to respond to potential situations:

When Qantas closed down for four days, we had clients that had to fly into Bangkok using them, so all we could do is to come into the office, find out who our clients were, produce a list of who was travelling, then call them up and say this is the situation.

Effective crisis communication – especially internal communication – develops through regular practice and rehearsal. One tour operator cited the relationships with subsidiaries and ground operators fostered in each destination as a key factor for his increase in confidence that a crisis can effectively be dealt with; thanks to faster communication between the parties and a better understanding of expectations:

We have very good ground operators in Thailand and in the various countries; we work with operators who understand our procedures and how we think this situation should be dealt with. So we work in close partnership with local suppliers to ensure client safety especially in times of crisis.

External communication is also a key issue to address the need to strengthen it in order to prepare for the effects of possible political crises. Social media has become one of the main external communication channels for customers and other stakeholders, as they are often readily accessible and reach a large audience in a short time:

If a political crisis happens, we do have plans to deal with it through social communication, which is a lot quicker nowadays. People are now relying more on social media sites like Twitter, Facebook, bloggers, etc. Not only that, they can actually view things more online, but we can put our own perspective [sic] behind it. And we are on Twitter and Facebook... we're getting ourselves more in line with paper advertising, as well. It has been very good for us and people actually trust us knowing what we're doing so we've got very good communications with TAT and with other airline partners as well.

Various channels of communication were cited by the interviewees, including direct contact, traditional media outlets and social media platforms. Differing channels of communication play unique roles in terms of external communication. The interviewees believe that strengthening outside communication is critical, as it can convey security information both to tourists and broader audiences in times of unfolding events.

MARKET SEGMENTATION

Some organisations implement a market segmentation strategy to plan effectively for future political crises. Such strategies take into account how the image of an affected destination may vary depending on the view of a given tourist segment. Some tourist segments are enormously affected by a particular crisis, whereas others are not at all.

This market segmentation strategy can include behavioural segmentation. Customers are divided into groups according to their knowledge of a tourism product or destination, their experiences with it and their attitudes towards it. The experienced tourist segment is generally better prepared for the possible effects of political crisis; this is due to their higher level of understanding a location and culture of a destination.

One tour operator explained that her company had expanded to a new segment of tourists who are both more mature and experienced in travelling, thus rendering them less sensitive to some of the effects of political crises and media perceptions; they are often better equipped to discern the threats and safety levels of a destination on their own. This group is less likely to be significantly affected by the news media or lack of confidence. Incorrect or distorted perceptions similarly do not make a large impact on them:

One of the factors is that [our] Thailand customers are mainly experienced travellers. The target market for Thailand is a more educated, more informed traveller and as a consequence of the market in Thailand being of that nature, they are perhaps more used to turmoil and the recovery of turmoil. And I also think the experienced UK customer is quite pragmatic and they tend to be jaded by the press being dramatic or by situations causing challenges. They rebound quite quickly.

Implementation of a market segmentation strategy is an important means of preparing for the unexpected. Expanding into a more sophisticated clientele segment which is less sensitive to the effects of political crises and perceptions developed by the media at large is one way to mitigate risks.

CRISIS RESPONSE STRATEGIES

Crisis response strategies fall into three main areas: (1) operational response, whereby immediate actions are implemented in order to deal with the effects of a political crisis impacting customers and suppliers within the first 48 hours; (2) marketing response, through which short-term marketing strategies are implemented to offset the loss of current and future sales; and (3) financial response.

OPERATIONAL RESPONSE

This strategy varies depending on whether the customers include tourists, tour operators, travel agents or destination organisations. For example, destination organisations may first contact the tourism board of the affected destination to stay updated and monitor the crisis; then they can relay the information to trade tourism organisations, tour operators and travel agents serving the region. By contrast, the tour operators' immediate response is to locate all their customers at the affected destination and evacuate them from the area if necessary:

We immediately contact our service providers out there, because it's a lot to do with how they coping. Because they are like our front line, because they look after our clients, obviously they will be the one [sic] that's helping us or how they can [sic] cooperate with us and hotels that we have to work as a team. The first contact will be the hotel and also the way we communicate between us makes a lot of difference as to how are we make the decision.

This response shows that tourism consultants and tour operators implement different approaches in the face of crises. Therefore, it is critical to identify the unique responses within the industry such as those that exist between tour operators, their clients and their service providers, with the destination.

The interaction of the tourists and the destination providers with the stakeholders in the originating market are either direct or indirect. This is important as it affects the effectiveness of the response to crises. Tourists include customers in the affected destination and those scheduled to travel to it. Service providers at the affected destination are those providing services to travellers, including ground operators, transportation and hospitality. The table below show the interaction between the affected parties:

TABLE 9.1 INTERACTION BETWEEN STAKEHOLDERS AND TOURISTS

Tourism sector	Tourists	Destination providers
Tour operators	Direct	Direct
Travel agents	Direct	Indirect
Destination organisations	Indirect	Direct
Tourism consultants	Indirect	Indirect

As the table shows, tour operators and travel agents uncompromisingly respond to crisis situations by contacting their tourist customers in the area. While operators respond directly to destination providers, agents act only as intermediaries between tourists and providers without direct contact with the latter. Tourism consultants do not respond directly with neither the tourists or the destination providers, however they do respond directly to tour operators and travel agents in the originating market, providing advice during a crisis. Finally, destination organisations may also indirectly respond to tourists, however their crucial task is to directly respond to the stakeholders in the originating markets.

In the case of a wholesale tour operator who sells tours to UK travel agents, they said they were additionally responsible for contacting all customers during times of crisis:

You have to deal first and foremost with your clients who are on the ground, so our focus is on people who are already in the destination that is affected. If we, as a tour operator, didn't show that duty of care, the retailer or travel agents would lose confidence in us as an operator. So this is very important regardless of where in the world a political crisis happens. We take the initiative in that we show we are in control of the situation and we respond positively to make sure all customers are taken as a priority; and the travel agents would see that and trust that we're a reputable tour operator and that we are capable of handling such issues in a positive way.

Tour operators play a more important role than their trade counterparts (consultants, travel agents and destination organisation personnel) in terms of their immediate and direct response to political crises. Understanding how different trade organisations respond and interact with one another in times of crisis is a necessary part of crisis management.

Tour operators typically employ a four-stage operational response spanning the first forty-eight hours and the immediate days following the crisis. This is illustrated in the table below:

TABLE 9.2 STAGES OF CRISIS OPERATIONAL RESPONSES

Tourists at destination	Tourists scheduled to travel	Destination providers
Stage 1: Compile and update the crisis situation		
Locate all guests	Prepare statement	Contact hotels and airlines
Stage 2: Evaluate crisis situation by levels of severity.		
Communicate with guests about the crisis situation	Update crisis situation and travel status by email or phone availability	Maintain contact about guests' safety and evacuation
Stage 3: Provide response to all stakeholders.		
Suggest evacuation if warranted	Inform about cancellations or delay	Communicate and coordinate evacuation logistics if warranted
After 48 hours: Maintain strong contact with all customers.		
Evacuate and continue to communicate	Maintain contact and support to change or delay travel plans	Negotiate cancellation of upcoming bookings

The moment a political crisis occurs, tour operators consult different sources of information to provide an update of the situation. Their sources include ground operators, news channels, other media, the Foreign and Commonwealth Office (FCO), and travel blogs:

111

If a crisis is happening in Burma, the first thing I will do will be to talk to our local office in Burma, and make sure, find out where they are. They normally have a guide with them or their own private guide, private driver. Make sure that they have a guide with them.

During this stage, they locate all customers, along with the hotels they are staying in and the airlines they are scheduled to fly on:

Immediately what we would do is to look at all the customers we have in a resort and look at all the customers that are due to travel imminently and we'll deal with them separately. Obviously our priorities are to look after anybody that is already in the country and it's often quite difficult to understand the situation when you're suddenly put into it and you have to make very quick decisions, which in hindsight, may not always be entirely the right decision. But the main thing is, you know, you always have to focus on your customers' safety and making the best decisions for them.

Some operators may also prepare additional crisis information for those customers scheduled to travel to the affected destination in the near future.

The second stage occurs when updates on the crisis are received from business partners. They may reconcile this information with travel warnings from the FCO website in order to decide the best course of action for assisting customers. Most operators view FCO advice as an essential source of crisis communication, particularly because it directly affects insurance coverage for customers. Once the crisis is evaluated, they may issue a letter or email to their prospective customers or they may choose to communicate directly with their customers at this time (both those currently travelling at the affected destination and those scheduled to travel to it):

We would monitor what the Foreign and Commonwealth Office (FCO) says. We will run a report to see if we have clients that are due to travel from now until the end of the year at least, and decide depending on the advice of the Foreign and Commonwealth office whether we stop clients from travelling to Burma or not; and this also depends on how soon the first batch of clients would be going to the country. And then we would contact the clients, talk to them about the situation, about their options and assure them that we are monitoring the situation and that we will make decisions that ensure their safety. Sometimes we may have to postpone tours and sometimes we would have to cancel all of them together [sic] and we can also offer alternative holidays for them; and if they wish they can re-book at a later date to go to Burma.

Tour operators may also contact hotel suppliers regarding the safety of their guests, while tracking airline press releases to provide updates. At this point they also track changes in airlines' cancellation policies and seat availability so that they can proactively plan should an evacuation or flight re-scheduling occurs:

After I talk to our local office, I would try to always call them, maybe at their hotel, to explain what's going on and see how we can best handle our customers; whether they need to take a domestic flight or re-route their flights back home. I would talk to our flight consolidator about, say, if they need to leave the country straight away, how we would change their flight and how much it would cost. After that, in a lot of situations, the travel insurance will cover the cost of that, so I'll ask the client to talk to their travel insurance as well.

Once they have carefully evaluated all information, the third stage begins. Action taken depends on the severity of the crisis and any financial constraints. They may also communicate with stakeholders such as hoteliers or airlines at this time:

We need to talk with hotel management regarding aspects such as room cancellation or extension of stay. Airline partners are also contacted, particularly if an evacuation is required, as in this case all customers would need to be accommodated on available flights as soon as possible.

Customer safety is the number one priority, but financial repercussions must be considered as well. This is in large part due to consumer protection laws by which organisations are legally bound.

The crisis in Egypt is a good example. The demonstrations occurred primarily in Cairo and the conflict was domestic, pitting the Egyptian demonstrators against their own government. However, cities throughout the country were deemed unsafe because of the risk of a spillover effect. An FCO advisory affected customers who had purchased travel insurance but had not yet departed for Egypt, as such an advisory suspends all future travel insurance to the affected area. Therefore operators encouraged their customers to evacuate Egypt, even if they were not likely to be directly affected by the unfolding crisis; this was with financial considerations in mind, as unrelated accidents such as falls or injuries would not be covered by insurance policies any longer. With exposure to both practical and financial risks, the organisation can ultimately minimise its liability by recommending that all customers should leave the country as soon as practical:

When the Foreign Commonwealth Office advised against all but essential travel to Egypt, we immediately located all the customers in the resorts and looked at all the customers due to travel in the near term and dealt with them separately. For the beach resorts and places like Luxor, it wasn't as bad but obviously in Cairo that was the main focus of all the demonstration and that's where we decided that it was important for all our customers to be kept in a safe place and then brought home as quickly as possible.

If evacuation is advised and customers decline this, a disclaimer needs to be signed by customers at this stage:

What is interesting is that often customers don't want to move. They are aware of what's happening on the ground and they can see that it doesn't affect them specifically where they are staying, and so they think, 'why do I have to move?' So we give them the choice: we say well, you have the opportunity to move or if you want to stay we just need you to sign a waiver or disclaimer to say that we've given you the opportunity to move and you've chosen not to do that.

In the case of customers who are scheduled to travel, the operators contact them to enquire whether they wish to change their destination or cancel their holiday altogether. If the situation is not perceived as dangerous, most operators suggest amending an itinerary by omitting the affected area. If, however, the situation is perceived as unsafe the scheduled tour is typically cancelled and customers are provided a full refund.

During this third stage they may also communicate with

hotel management regarding room cancellations or extension of stays. Airline partners are likewise contacted to prepare for the possibility of an evacuation.

The fourth and final stage is the period after the first forty-eight hours. After the crisis response plan is implemented, the operators then ensure all customers are in safe locations and maintain close levels of contact with them to keep them abreast of the latest developments. For those customers scheduled to travel to an affected destination in the near future, where a decision to postpone the destination has been agreed between the parties, the operators continue to provide regular situation updates. If, on the other hand, the decision to cancel the tour has been made, it is the responsibility of the tourism organisations to negotiate customer refunds with their suppliers (i.e. airlines and hotels). When suppliers help to absorb such cancellation costs, the financial fallout from a crisis on a tourism organisation can be greatly reduced.

In Thailand, hotels' cancellation policies are better than some other destinations. For example, we had a situation in South Africa where because of the Icelandic volcano Heathrow [Airport] was closed for a week and hotels in South Africa that we had prepaid said 'no, you can't have any money back for full cancellation', but in Thailand they are more accommodating.

MARKETING RESPONSE

Short-lived and long-lived political crises require distinct marketing responses. A short-lived crisis is generally acknowledged to last less than 72 hours, while beyond that point it is considered to be long-lived. Developing an appropriate marketing strategy and actions for a long-lived crisis can be difficult when the direction of a crisis remains unclear:

Yes, the long-lived crisis is more difficult to respond to than the one-day incidents as it depends on the severity of the incidents and what incidents have happened in the past. And fortunately, because the tourism industry is very competitive, if a long-lived crisis happens it is difficult to come back. As a result, tour operators shift marketing campaigns to other destinations that are more mature and stable instead of the politically unstable destination.

The following table summarises marketing responses to the effects of both types of crises. While the responses are mainly temporary suspensions of marketing and emphasis to alternative destinations during short-lived crises, the marketing responses to long-lived ones are lasting, with removal of products and development of marketing to alternative destinations.

TABLE 9.3 MARKETING RESPONSE STRATEGIES

	Effects	Marketing responses
Short-lived crises	Cancellation of upcoming bookings	Suspend marketing of the affected destination and enhance marketing of unaffected destinations
Long-lived crises	Overall sales of particular destinations	Substitute affected destinations with alternate destinations of similar marketing characteristics

Given that political crises affect organisations through cancellations of new and existing reservations, the immediate response in terms of marketing is to suspend marketing of the location altogether, as demand falls precipitously following a crisis event. In this situation, there is no point in spending money on marketing products to that particular region.

If there is a military coup [in Thailand] tomorrow, I've got to say that I would immediately divert all resources away from marketing because there's no point; it is completely an uphill battle. No one listens. You can do all the marketing you like, but if it's say on the BBC News that there's a military coup, there is no way you are going to get any new bookings to Thailand.

In some cases, tourism organisations may have to decline services to customers requesting travel to affected destinations. Operators generally discourage travel to affected regions for a time until normality is restored. Some crises, such as the prolonged protests in Thailand, the crisis in Egypt and the Libyan Revolution, occur over a longer time frame. Such long-lived crises require unique marketing strategies; the longer a crisis features in the media, the greater the damage to a destination's image. One operator explained the process of removing a destination suffering from long-lived crises from its product inventories:

The main criterion for taking out such products is firstly that the business must have been affected for a long period of time and the destination must be perceived as an unsafe destination. So, taking any product off is a very long-term decision; we have to wait for at least a year, or even more, before we take the decision.

In cases where an affected destination's image deteriorates over an extended period of time, other destinations with similar features and interests are then selected to market to their customers. In the case of Egypt, customers may be encouraged to visit Petra in Jordan instead, as it offers similar ancient and archaeological sites to explore.

Taking all this into account, it is evident that crisis marketing can occur during and immediately following a political crisis. Such is the case with short-term strategy and in the long-term, which involves recovery strategies for the purpose of organisational recovery.

FINANCIAL STRATEGIES

Loss of revenue affects organisations during and after political crises through reduced bookings, cancellations and in some cases the complete collapse of demand for a particular destination. Organisations may also incur unexpected and considerable expenses as a result of assisting customers in an impacted area.

It is imperative for organisations to apply financial strategies to mitigate the effects of crises after the severity of the situation has been evaluated. This is done by assessing the level of financial exposure against the reserves set aside for such contingencies. If a crisis continues over a long period, perceptions of insecurity can increase, eroding customer confidence. This can result in profound financial consequences, as related by one tour operator:

Importantly, continuous political crises may cause tourism companies high financial costs in order to support their customers who are in the affected areas: these may include refunds, ticket amendments, and cancellation charges. As a result, the company might be unable to continue their business.

Organizations need to estimate the various potential expenses, including operational response costs (such as those for hotel and flight cancellations or re-routing itineraries), marketing loss and lost sales opportunities. Anticipating these costs as soon as possible helps an organisation to manage its cash flow and absorb the extra expenditure entailed.

Non-essential expenditure may be suspended or removed during a crisis. However, such reductions can affect the image of an organisation and accordingly must be weighed carefully. For example, lowering the quality of brochures to save on marketing costs may result in long-term damage to an organisation's brand image. Similarly, cancelling the marketing campaign for a particular destination can save money in the short term but may damage it in the long term, as reflected by a travel consultant:

Our company provides marketing consultant services to hotels in Thailand. During the Thai protests in 2010, a few of these clients decided they needed to save on the cost of marketing by eliminating this budget and using the savings for other things. It took about three to four months for them to come back and use our marketing service again and I do think it is a backward situation, as the affected Thai hotels should maintain marketing to ensure their hotels' visibility, especially during and after crises.

Thus, such a cost reduction strategy requires very careful consideration and implementation to ensure that healthy areas of the business are not negatively and unnecessarily affected.

Another potential strategy for cost control involves negotiating with tourism stakeholders. During the floods in

Bangkok in 2011, airlines and hotels reduced or eliminated cancellation costs. A tour operator explained how this helped to curb their losses:

An example is probably the bad weather [resulting in the floods] in Bangkok last year; airlines were very quick to make sure that customers did not feel dissatisfied. So we did make some full cancellations and also rescheduled their holidays; even the hotels were very good, offering free changes. There was actually such availability of flights and hotels at no extra cost for the customers that the customers could still go back later - up to a year later - to visit Thailand as planned; or if they couldn't do this because their dates were fixed, we offered them a full refund which was no problem.

It is also important for organisations to review their financial status against the potential effects of political incidents in order to anticipate exposure over the course of the subsequent three to six months; they should then set a contingency budget that reflects these revelations. Ultimately, financial considerations are critical for the continuity of an organisation during times of political crisis. Financial responses, of course, need to be implemented in accordance with marketing responses during times of crisis, while operational responses require immediate execution.

FACTORS AFFECTING RESPONSE

Response to a crisis depends upon multiple factors, including the degree of violence, the duration of the crisis, the characteristics of the affected destination, the coincidence of several crises, the timing of a political crisis and the degree of media interest.

Most organisations have encountered adverse effects due to political crises, such as the Sri Lankan Civil War, the Bali bombings, the Arab Spring, the protests in Thailand, the Burmese monk demonstrations and strikes in India. During the Arab Spring and Thai demonstrations, Most tourists were evacuated from the affected destinations. Other examples abound, like this one from an operator:

I used to deal with Egypt and there was a big terrorist attack in Luxor in 1997. Our company actually lost tourists in that attack and that's probably the most difficult thing in my whole career. The company had 300 people in Egypt at that time. We were talking over the phone to the Foreign Office and every passenger had to be evacuated in 48 hours, so the company had to send the plane, gather all our passengers and fly them out within 48 hours. The impact was enormous. Tourism didn't recover probably for two years after that and actually, to be honest, probably never got back to where it was in those days because there have been some smaller incidents since that time.

The duration of a political crisis and the awareness that non-violent events can become violent over time also influence decisions:

The factor for consideration is the length of the time it lasted. I think if it does last a very long time then it can be very damaging. For the Thai political situation in 2010, it was difficult because it slowly grew. We actually made judgements day by day and on that level.

The 2010 political protest in Thailand, which affected a great numbers of stakeholders, began as a non-violent protest but escalated over the course of some months, culminating in an incident which triggered the country's worst political crisis of the decade. This case illustrates how even non-violent situations can evolve into violent confrontations; tourism organisations need to be well aware of such situations and plan accordingly for the possible effects.

Organisations must also take into account the characteristics of the affected destination, including the historical roots of political crises and the infrastructure. The importance of Thailand's strong infrastructure was a main factor supporting the tourism industry after the post-crisis period. It allowed the destination to be resilient in the face of recurring crises:

The history of political crises of each country affects perception differently; protests in Egypt would have a hundred times more effect than protests in Bangkok.

The coincidence of several crises at once can also affect the tourism industry. As mentioned above, the simultaneous occurrence of the volcanic eruption in Iceland in April 2010 followed immediately by the red-yellow shirts demonstration in Thailand of May 2010 disrupted the UK's tourism industry. Such situations with multiple adverse events have a greater effect on the tourism industry than those that occur in isolation:

The political problem in Thailand coincided with the natural events of the volcano in Iceland closing European airports, so we have people stuck in Bangkok who wanted to leave but couldn't because there were no flights. This was such big news that it was the first time I've seen a drop and then a continued drop in the number of tourists enquiring and travelling and I see that now... even now.

Another important factor is the timing of a political crisis. The effects are greater if it occurs during the holiday season than during off-peak times. Likewise, media response to a crisis also affects the tourism industry. Media reports during crises often tend to exaggerate the effects:

The media are important as well because of how they report the situation, and there are some things that happen that do not register with the media. But there are certain things that media are just not interested in. An example of this was a case when I used to look after Africa, and I was travelling to Kenya at the election time several years ago. Almost anything that happened would make quite prominent news even if it was relatively small in terms of the wider scale of things. I think that because of the historical links between the UK and Kenya, and also because I know that Nairobi is a hub for correspondents in Africa, there are lots of journalists actually based there who are looking for something to report. And that's often the case where you find situations that generate more news in one place than they would if they happened somewhere else.

CRISIS RECOVERY STRATEGIES

Confidence is key to the crisis recovery process. If the affected destination regains confidence quickly, the tourism industry can recuperate, helping organisations also recover from loss of sales. Crisis recovery strategies serve as essential elements of crisis management, helping to restore tourist and stakeholder confidence in affected destinations. While most organisations implement marketing recovery strategies following periods of crisis, some may elect to abandon the affected destination and shift resources to other unaffected areas. This is especially true for travel agents who typically market a large number of destinations:

I don't really have one [strategy]. We just let the situation calm down. We've got a lot of destinations anyway so people who are going to Thailand get sent to Malaysia, Bali or Vietnam instead.

All stakeholders play an equally important role in terms of the collaborative effort required during a recovery, as this comment from a tour operator indicates:

I think that is a collaborative effort between the government of the destination through the tourism board and commercial partners who support tourism in the destination ... no one stakeholder can influence recovery in tourism and I think it's the value of the tourism board that can be measured by its ability to coordinate and galvanise the tourism industry to that recovery effort.

Each stakeholder has its own unique part to execute, such as the publication of brochures or communications of reassurance to clients and partners. Travel agents assist when they return the affected destination to their list of products, while hoteliers and airline partners launch campaigns to attract tourists with or without discounted prices. The government's marketing and promotional campaigns, along with regular press releases, are highly visible and significant to attracting tourism back to an area. As a consequence, once tourism to the affected destination resumes, awareness of and confidence in its safety gradually restores itself in many cases. Thus, each stakeholder serves an important role within the collaborative process:

Everybody helps to promote [the destination]. Considering who is the most important, each part has their own place: the media; the tourism office have the responsibility of promoting the destination being a safe place; and the tour company like us and ground handlers have the responsibility of giving tours at good value so the price will be better. All of them have to work together.

Marketing strategies can be categorised into two main areas: (1) private sector, including tour operators, travel agents, service providers (e.g. hotels, airlines) and media, and (2) public sector including the tourism board, government, tourism organisations (e.g. ABTA, PATA).

The key marketing strategies can be summarised as a list:

Private sector strategies:

- Media trips to the recovering destination
- Price reductions and promotions
- Start marketing from the beginning again with fresh content
- Emphasis online and social media for quicker results
- Collaboration with other stakeholders such as airlines, hospitality, tour operators and the media
- Rebuild a positive image through the media

Public sector strategies:

- Increase frequency of press release with latest updates
- Increase contact with the media to improve image
- Familiarisation trips offered to stakeholders in generating markets

PRIVATE SECTOR STRATEGIES

The private sector, which includes tour operators, travel agents, service providers (i.e. hotels and airlines) and media, plays a significant role in shortening a crisis recovery period.

One of the recovery strategies is media trips, sending journalists to the affected destination; this is done to bring trusted first-hand reports and visuals to the consumers to show that it is once again safe to travel to a destination. Media trips usually involve travel trade journalists such as *Condé Nast Traveller* or the travel sections of newspapers like *The Guardian* or *The Sunday Times* as well as television channels:

We have a strategy or plan to deal with the recovery period. We usually tend to have a promotion for that region. We invest in marketing by sending journalists and writing about the destination to cover the media, newspapers and magazines. Most of the hotels are always helpful about this.

Tour operators also communicate with their customers and travel agents to reinforce the message that the affected destination is safe, thereby encouraging them to consider it again as a destination:

Basically, trying to improve planning and customer awareness of the fact that the place is safe again... that's the main message that we have to try and get across and work together as a unit really.

Price reduction strategies through support from other stakeholders such as tourism boards, airlines, the media and hotels are also considered. By coordinating different service elements with which to formulate attractive tour packages, they can work in unison to promote the affected destination post-crisis:

In some political crisis situations, organisations find it easier to market affected destinations anew:

In the cases of political crises we had with Thailand, we started everything from the beginning so we had to start marketing the destination, promoting the destination and the company with online marketing. You start building up, and then people start looking at websites about Thailand again.

For the private sector, the hotel tends to throw in some promotion as well by value-added offers such as free nights, because they want to bring back the business and make sure it kicks back to life again.

Other tour operators also work very closely with hotel suppliers, because they are all trying to bring back tourists. What they do is give special offers to travel to pass on back to here and give benefits back to clients.

After the 2010 crisis, the Thai tourism industry worked closely with stakeholders in the United Kingdom; in particular, a solid collaborative effort developed between the industry, the country's national airline, Thai Airways, and the tourism-generating UK. The airline offered discounted tickets for travel to Thailand following the crisis. Such collaboration can help to improve the image of the affected destination:

The Thailand Tourism Authority had been good at promoting Thailand after the crisis, particularly through Thai Airways. It's quite a strong brand. Also, they have promotional materials such as maps and things like that. I think that people really do recognise the image of Thailand from the Thai Tourism Authority and Thai airways, so promotion has been quite effective.

Another strategy is to attract new or different segments of the tourist population. Experienced travellers are particularly prized as their confidence tends to suffer less from misgivings towards a destination post-crisis, so they play a crucial role during the recovery process.

The media are most useful during this phase. Marketing recovery strategies in collaboration with the media can be categorised as follows:

(1) General media: the BBC, TV, regular newspapers (mainly for the public),

(2) Specialised media: travel and leisure media, e.g. *Condé Nast Traveller* (mainly for the public), and

(3) Trade media: the TGG, *Travel Daily* (mainly for trade stakeholders).

Tour operators typically leverage general media to rebuild tourist confidence, as it targets a wide, general audience, whereas specialised media defines and fine-tunes the image to more of a niche audience:

I guess, actually after the crisis the media do play a role, because if people see positive images about the place on the news or they see things like that on TV about places changing, I think that does sort of play in people's mind and makes them want to go.

Trade media are business-to-business, focusing on trade organisations to enhance awareness of the image of affected destinations. Some organisations often coordinates with trade media to provide marketing and advertising for an affected destination:

To restore confidence, we also work closely with other trade media in the UK, for example TGG or Travel Bulletin. We have to say to the media that look, it is okay now in Thailand. These are people who spread the news within the industry. Obviously, they are the first to get the news and agents pass news back to the consumers. For the media, it's a combination of all those actually. Because I think for some reason any bad news comes out from the BBC quicker than from anywhere else.

PUBLIC SECTOR STRATEGIES

Where the tourism industry is concerned, the public sector refers to tourism boards and government and tourism organisations (e.g. ABTA, PATA). The public sector serves an important role in the crisis recovery period:

In the recovery process, I would involve the tourism office and we'll have our retail offices, so we might involve them in doing promotions with the tourism board. Have special offers as well. Specially priced holidays will come out to try and promote the destination and that is the sort of thing we would promote and advertise to try and let our clients know that the destination is ready for people to return and then encouraging people by offering some special discounts, special prices, and airlines as well. Something like Egypt Air would look at encouraging travel again, so again, they might be bringing out special prices on their air fares as well. It's very much a joint effort to try and encourage in recovery.

Tourism boards' main function is to help local businesses attract more attention in international markets. They play a crucial role in communicating with a broad audience, thus restoring a destination's image and increasing stakeholder confidence. Accordingly, they organise marketing campaigns that are supported not only by the government but by local businesses such as hotels.

Tourism boards carry the most influence in terms of the image of a country following a crisis; these boards need the support of tour operators and travel agents in order to once again establish confidence in their destinations:

I think it is very important for tourism boards to invest in positive PR and positive marketing to encourage the broader market to have confidence in the destination again, and they do it in partnership with the airlines or the hotels in order to reassure people that the market is back to normal. It's quite important for relationships with travel agents.

Tourism boards also provide regular press releases and updates:

My opinion about the TAT office is that they should give regular press releases and updates to the press as to what the situation is, as a lot of times different media companies have their own perceptions of what the situation is like, so if there is an official statement on a very regular basis by the tourism authority of Thailand in Thailand itself this is likely to have a significant effect on public perception. While at the moment, it's very random as everybody takes their own guess as how long [crises] will last.

Governments play an integral role in restoring confidence to an affected destination after the crisis has past. Thus, if tourism boards and governments implement proper recovery marketing strategies, they can help to minimise the length of crisis recovery.

For example, after the 2010 crisis, the Thai government, through its tourism board and the Tourism Authority of Thailand in London, worked with stakeholders including airlines, the media, and trade organisations to restore investor confidence; press trips were then organised and UK tourism managers, journalists and travel consultants visited Thailand to see for themselves:

The TAT office invited the tour operators from the UK and Ireland to go to different places in Thailand to see the suppliers instead of going to the travel mart. And also, we use PR to get the news out of the country that Thailand is safe and this is what we all hear. A lot of buyers from the UK and Ireland went there and used the opportunity to make lots of news to spread throughout mainland Europe that Thailand is safe.

For crisis recovery strategies to be most effective, they also must be implemented at the right moment:

When the problem is over, then you launch the recovery plan to encourage people to come back. What's important is the timing. Give a little time for people to settle.

The government's role is also to ensure the destination is ready to accept tourists once again. This is especially true for locations affected by war, which often damages a great deal of the infrastructure necessary for tourism. In such cases, the restoration period needs to be taken into consideration before strategic crisis recovery plans can be implemented.

SUMMARY

Although the effects of political crises cannot be altogether avoided, they can be mitigated if trade organisations put proper strategies into place beforehand that include risk reduction, perception assessments and travel insurance. Of particular significance is the strategy of diversification of tourism products, which assists in maintaining the continuity of an organisation, should a political crisis disrupt business; by ensuring that it is not too heavily dependent upon any particular destination, a business can spread its risk over multiple locations. Additionally, communication can be strengthened in advance to ensure that information is conveyed effectively at the time of a crisis. Together with behaviour segmentation, a market segmentation strategy is further recommended, as it allows trade organisations to select consumer markets which fare comparatively well during political crises.

CHAPTER 10

TOWARDS THE FUTURE

An effective political crisis response framework involves work in three main areas. First, we need to classify political crises. Second, the contributions of different sources of information in times of crises have to be considered. Finally a framework of political crisis responses have to be developed for the tourism industry.

TYPOLOGY OF POLITICAL CRISES

There are four characteristics of political crises that require consideration:

- The roots of conflicts
- Management control
- Disruption
- Cultural differences.

There is a lack of consensus in the tourism literature over the definition of the term 'political crisis' (as it applies to the tourism industry), where the term 'political instability' is also often used instead. For example, acts of terrorism may not constitute a political crisis when they originate from external factors. However, given that the effects and crisis management response to terrorism are in many ways similar to those of political crises, this book retains terrorism within its scope.

On the other hand, environmental crises, such as the Thailand floods of 2011, may be considered political crises, because of the management control aspect of such events.

In addition, cultural differences can account for varying perceptions and thus are an important factor to consider. A political incident may be perceived as a political crisis by onlookers in one country, but not in another. This helps to explain why tourism literature lacks consensus on the use of the term 'political crisis' as historically, disruptive events affecting some destinations may have referenced as political crises by some sources while not by others. This factor is a reason why the tourism industry lacks a structured political crisis management framework. Cultural differences appear to identify political crises differently, dependent upon social and geopolitical contexts.

The issues discussed above help us understand how political crises affect various tourism organisations, as the four characteristics are of great value to the tourism industry in the field of political crisis management which forms part of a political crisis response framework.

We suggest the following definition of political crisis:

Any incident or event originating from the management shortcomings of a destination's government which negatively affects organisations and the daily lives of people in the area, thereby potentially affecting the tourism industry; however, the effects of such situations can vary considerably as a result of cultural differences.

The effects of different types of political crises on the tourism industry may include perception effects, financial effects, effects in the aftermath, influences of coinciding effects and ripple and spillover effects. The perception effect is the single most important determinant of tourist confidence in the affected destination. The financial effect is a direct consequence of perception that occurs as a destination's image deteriorates. Consequently, destination image is the most significant factor requiring consideration when developing a political crisis management strategy.

This figure presents a method for understanding the nature of political crises. The two-dimensional figure includes four areas, each influenced by the combination of the degree of violence and the duration of the crisis. This distribution leads to different management approaches for each type of crisis event.

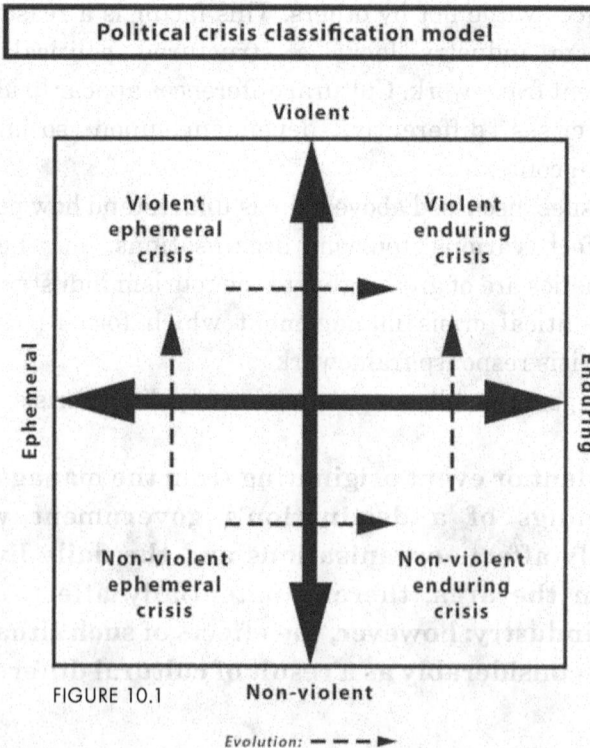

Political crisis classification model

Violent

Violent ephemeral crisis

Violent enduring crisis

Ephemeral

Enduring

Non-violent ephemeral crisis

Non-violent enduring crisis

FIGURE 10.1   Non-violent

Evolution: ▬ ▬ ▬ ▶

Political crisis situations can frequently be assessed in terms of the degree of violence involved and their duration, as expressed in the above figure. The first dimension is the degree of violence, which ranges from non-violent to violent. The second dimension is the duration of the crisis, which ranges from ephemeral to enduring, where ephemeral may span from a few hours to a few days and enduring from several days to months or even years. From these two dimensions, political crises can be divided into four main types: (1) violent enduring crises, (2) violent ephemeral crises, (3) non-violent enduring crises, and (4) non-violent ephemeral crises.

As the name suggests, violent enduring crises are violent crisis events spanning a relatively long period. Examples of such crises are the Sri Lankan Civil War (1983-2009), the Burmese Monk Protest (2007), the Kashmir conflict (2010), the Egyptian Revolution (2011) and the Syrian civil war (2011-present). Enduring crises profoundly impact a destination's image because of sustained media coverage and, potentially, an over-emphasis on the dangers posed.

A violent enduring crisis can develop from a non-violent ephemeral crisis, a non-violent enduring crisis or a violent ephemeral crisis. Management responses may include evacuation of tourists from the immediate and surrounding areas. In terms of marketing response, the affected destinations are taken off sale.

Violent enduring crises can pose catastrophic challenges to the tourism industry as they can destroy tourists' perceptions of a country's safety for many years to come. An example of this is the long-lasting Gulf War in Iraq.

A violent ephemeral crisis stems from brief violent events. Examples of these are the Luxor Massacre (1997), the September 11 terrorist attacks (2001), the Bali Bombings (2002), the Manila Hostage Crisis (2011) and the Erawan bombing in Bangkok (2015). Different strategic responses apply to this type of crisis. Because of safety considerations caused by the higher degree of violence, the first course of action is to evacuate tourists from the affected area. Organisations can then suspend marketing of the affected destination.

A non-violent ephemeral crisis is a brief event, lasting from a few hours to a few days, which does not involve violence. Examples include the 24-hour Lufthansa strike in 2012, then again in 2015. Tourism stakeholders are typically less affected by such crises. In the Lufthansa case, tourism management responded by re-routing tourists to alternative flights. However, a non-violent ephemeral crisis can evolve into an enduring crisis which either remains non-violent or becomes violent.

Non-violent enduring crises can extend from several days to several months, as their name suggests, but remain non-violent. The protests in Greece (2010-2013) and the Bangkok Airport closure in 2008 are examples. Although they may appear to affect the tourism industry less, studies have shown that even non-violent enduring crises can have massive economic repercussions on the tourism economy of the region. When such an enduring crisis occurs, short-term sales strategies require adjustment by reworking tour itineraries to bypass affected areas. Marketing campaigns are similarly adjusted to feature alternative destinations within the same country. In the case of the Bangkok Airport closure, marketing campaigns were modified to exclude Bangkok in favour of Phuket, a beach destination far from Bangkok with its own international airport.

Non-violent enduring crises may or may not evolve into violent enduring crises. During the prolonged Thai protests in 2010, violence erupted in the tenth month following a single incident which spawned a succession of violent occurrences. From that point onwards, the incident was irreversibly perceived as a violent enduring crisis with far more severe consequences for tourism stakeholders. Tour operators evacuated customers from the entire country, marketing campaigns were altered, suspended or removed altogether and tour operators and travel agents in the tourist-generating regions stopped selling destinations in Thailand.

A political crisis classification model can facilitate organisations' crisis responses even when a crisis evolves into another type. However there is a limitation in using this model, as ephemeral crises can evolve into enduring events irrespective of the degree of violence. As it is difficult to foresee how crises will develop, and management response is required at an early stage when a crisis is still likely to be classified as ephemeral, the assessment of a crisis needs to be continuous and should evolve with the event, so as to provide for appropriate changes in response.

This classification model helps management to respond appropriately as events unfold. It can contribute to crisis management expertise by equipping tourism organisations with a better understanding of the appropriate response in various situations.

POLITICAL CRISES AND THE IMAGE-MAKING PROCESS MODEL

Communication during a crisis is of paramount concern. There are several different channels of crisis communication between the affected destination and stakeholders, especially those within the tourist-generating region, and it is important to understand how they are used to convey crisis information. Because most tourist-generating regions and destinations are geographically removed from one another and involve distinct cultures, the effects of crises can be magnified. There has been a significant amount of research conducted in destinations themselves, but far less attention has been paid to this issue in tourist-generating regions. In contrast, this book takes a fresh view of crisis management by drawing from primary data collected in a tourist-generating region (the United Kingdom); this leads to unique management approaches, which we will discuss in the next section.

An appreciation of image-making processes and how trade organisations and other stakeholders are informed about political crises provides a better understanding for tourism managers who are confronted with these situations.

The media are a fundamental source of crisis information. While media reports have an immediate effect on the image of a destination in times of political crisis, additional sources, such as crisis reporting through tourism trade organisations, destination organisations and ground operators, also intersect to form a broad picture of events. The emerging importance of social media in crisis information should not be overlooked, as the immediate impact of event reporting in social media may be even more significant to the general public than that of traditional media. Tourists also now receive instant information through social networks from different points around the world, thus dramatically altering the dynamics of crisis communication.

A broad spectrum of communication channels, including tourism trade organisations, destination organisations, ground operators, social media and traditional media, as well as their individual roles, needs to be included in crisis management. In addition, the way different sectors rely on different channels must be considered. Trade organisations in tourist-generating regions, such as tour operators, obtain more information from ground operators than they do from media coverage. These destination operators may readily confirm or disprove reports in the media, providing information support for crisis management. However, large organisations (those with more than 250 employees) tend to rely more on tourism trade organisations such as FTO as a source of communication in times of political crisis; they tend to have preferential contacts within these organisations who readily provide them with trustworthy information. Therefore, the most appropriate source of crisis information may depend upon the sector and the size of the distinct trade organisations involved.

The sources of crisis information mentioned here contribute to the crisis image-making model which is discussed further in the next sub-section. We will outline channels of communication that are important to trade organisations and other stakeholders in times of political crisis.

DESTINATION IMAGE AND CONFIDENCE

Three factors need to be considered with regard to the deterioration of a destination's image during times of political crises - geographical context, tourist segmentation and the destination government's own stability. In the first case, the ripple effect following a crisis affects the destination image of surrounding countries; for example the Syrian civil war affected travel to Iran, Saudi Arabia, Qatar, Bahrain, the United Arab Emirates and Oman. The Arab Spring is another example; here tourists avoided travelling to the entire Arab region. In the case of Thailand, tourists tended to avoid the whole south eastern region of Asia, although the crisis was confined to Bangkok.

Regarding tourist segmentation, perceptions differ depending upon the view of particular tourist segments. Experienced travellers are far better equipped to assess the real safety level of a particular destination than those who are less knowledgeable. This group is thus less likely to be affected by media reports, social media or loss of confidence among the wider public. Moreover, using Pearce's Travel Career Ladder model of 2011 as an example: "There are five hierarchical steps affecting tourist behaviour... relaxation, stimulation, relationship, self-esteem and development, and fulfilment"; experienced travellers pay less attention to safety and security issues than less experienced ones. This confirms that destination image plays a large role during political crises, as the subset of experienced travellers who are less affected is relatively small.

Finally, the ability of a destination's government to manage a crisis directly relates to both tourist confidence and destination image. If the government enjoys an overall positive image domestically and internationally with regard to its management of the situation, then the perception of safety at the destination will be less affected. Public perception of the government of a destination is, therefore, an important factor to consider during a political crisis, as its actions or statements can either improve or further damage the effects of political crises and how these are perceived.

The figure opposite shows the process by which crisis information is conveyed between the affected destination and the tourist-generating region. Also represented are the roles of governments and tourists. When political crises occur at tourism destinations, information is conveyed to stakeholders in the tourist-generating region through tourism trade organisations (e.g. ABTA, FTA), destination organisations (TAT), ground operators, the media (BBC, TV, social media) as well as through social media. As has been discussed in detail, political crises affect a destination image negatively; a degraded image damages stakeholder confidence in that particular destination. Government also plays a major role in communication between the two regions in addition to influencing the perception of the affected destination's image.

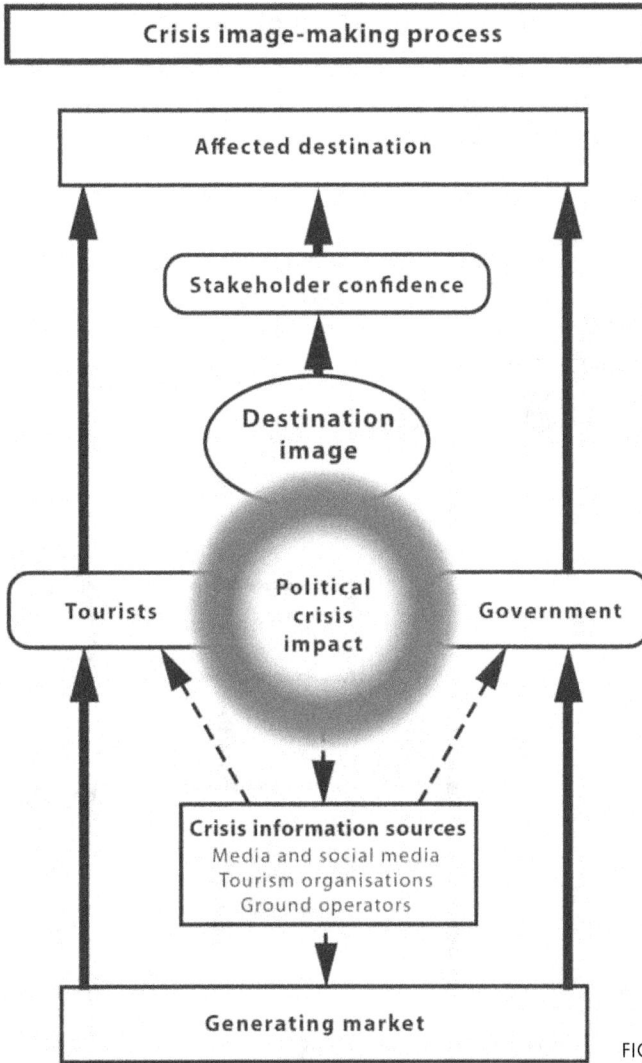

FIGURE 10.2

The model crisis image-making process demonstrates that the responses of stakeholders both within the affected destination and those in tourist-generating regions alongside the governments are determinant factors affecting the destination's image.

POLITICAL CRISIS STRATEGIES

There are five distinct phases to political crisis management, each influencing the next phase in a closed loop:

1. Mitigation
2. Preparedness
3. Response
4. Recovery
5. Organisational
   learning

Phases of political crisis management

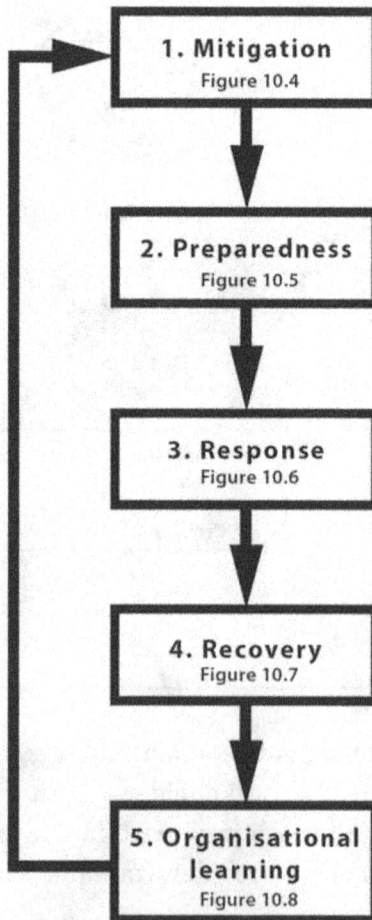

1. Mitigation
Figure 10.4

2. Preparedness
Figure 10.5

3. Response
Figure 10.6

4. Recovery
Figure 10.7

5. Organisational
learning
Figure 10.8

FIGURE 10.3

Political crisis strategies begin when organisations prepare ahead of time for possible effects by applying crisis mitigation strategies.

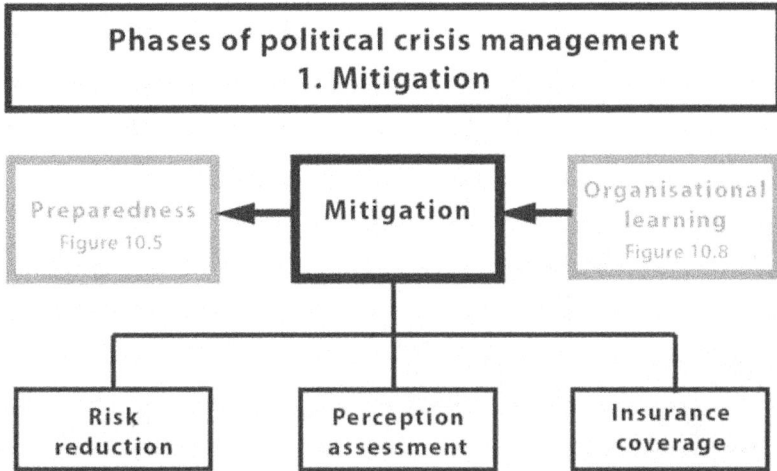

FIGURE 10.4

Preparedness strategies must be implemented before any crisis occurs.

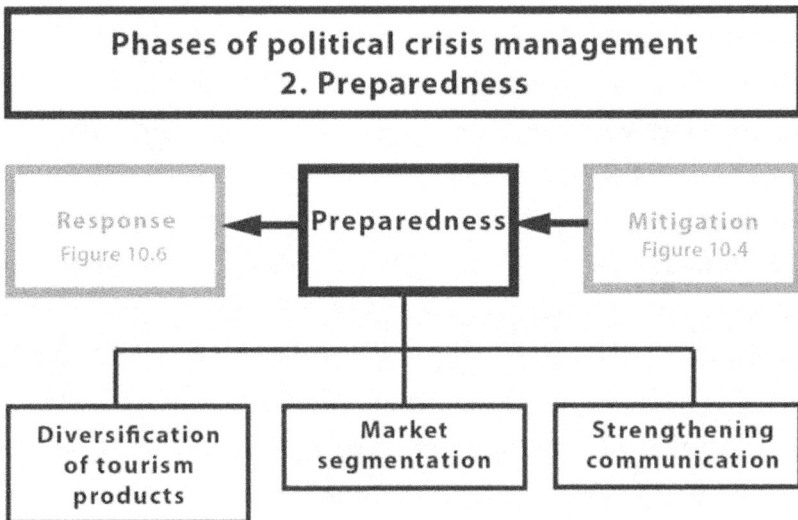

FIGURE 10.5

Once it strikes, the organisations then implement response strategies, executed according to the unique aspects of the management strategy (such as operational response, marketing response and financial response).

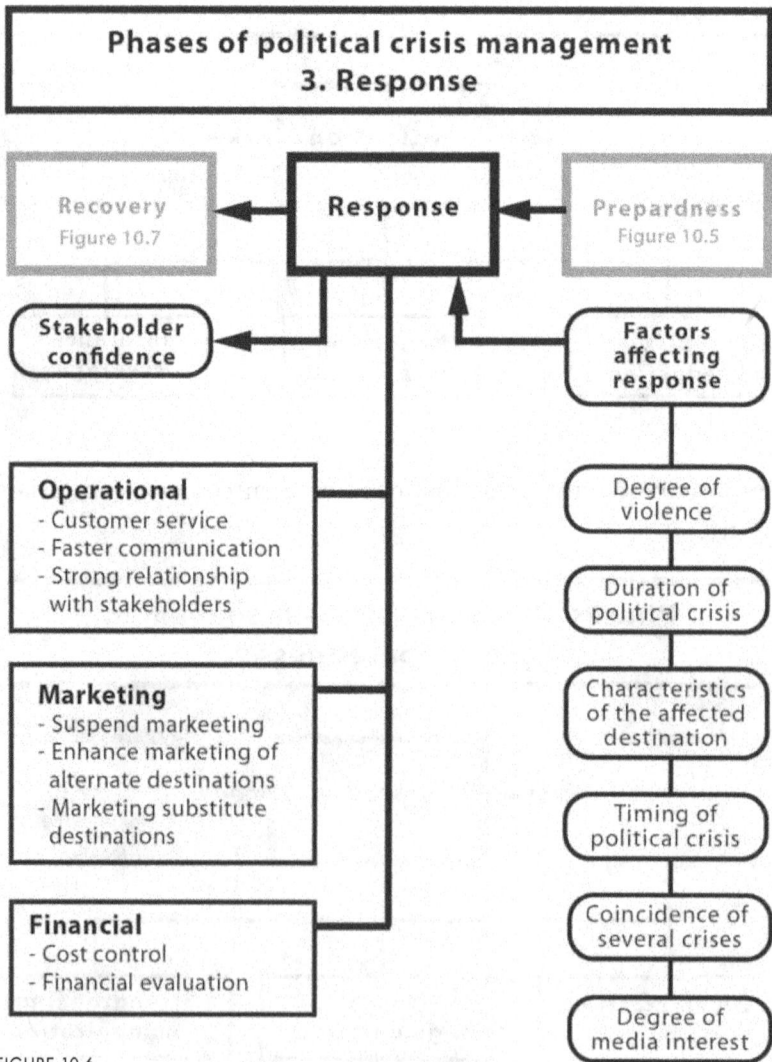

Phases of political crisis management
3. Response

Recovery Figure 10.7	**Response**	Prepardness Figure 10.5

Stakeholder confidence

Factors affecting response

Operational
- Customer service
- Faster communication
- Strong relationship with stakeholders

Degree of violence

Duration of political crisis

Marketing
- Suspend markeeting
- Enhance marketing of alternate destinations
- Marketing substitute destinations

Characteristics of the affected destination

Timing of political crisis

Financial
- Cost control
- Financial evaluation

Coincidence of several crises

Degree of media interest

FIGURE 10.6

146

After the crisis has ended, organisational stakeholders restore confidence in the affected destination by applying political crisis recovery strategies.

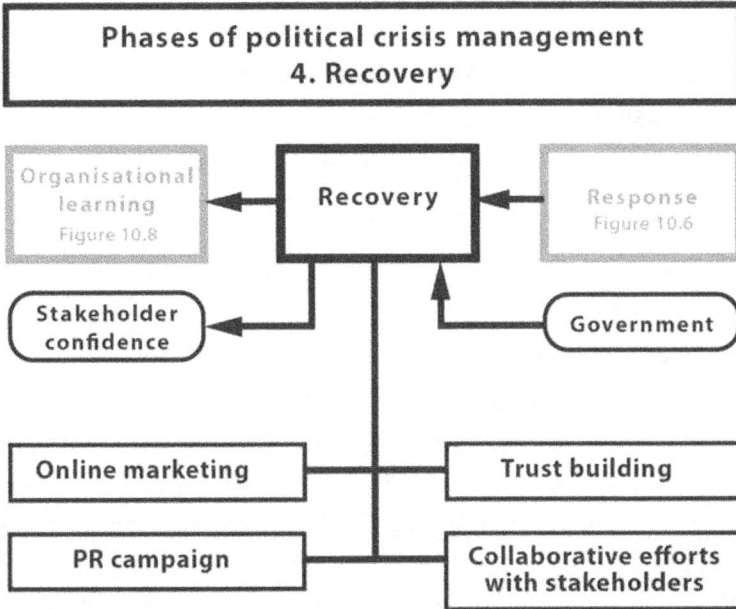

**Phases of political crisis management
4. Recovery**

FIGURE 10.7

They can then evaluate their existing strategies and make improvements to them during the organisational learning phase.

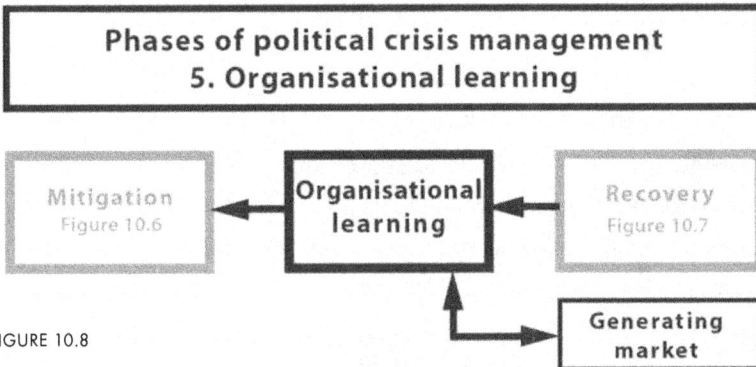

**Phases of political crisis management
5. Organisational learning**

FIGURE 10.8

Understandably, stakeholders believe political crises are more likely to occur where they have happened before. They prepare by learning from past crises and adopting appropriate strategies for future ones which may arise during the organisational learning phase.

Stakeholders in tourist-generating regions typically employ three strategies: risk reduction, perception assessment and insurance. The effects of political crises cannot be removed or avoided, so crisis mitigation strategies are essential to enable trade organisations to alleviate some of their effects.

Three additional strategies may also be implemented: diversification of tourism products, market segmentation and strengthening communication in times of crisis. There are two main considerations when implementing diversification strategy. The first is that diversification can be highly effective in reducing the effects of political crises and diverting existing clients to unaffected destinations. The second consideration is that diversification is a long and often expensive process, not without risks of its own; organisations must invest in knowledge and expertise as well as new products and relationships to leverage it effectively.

There is, of course, no guarantee of success. Thus, the potential benefits of this approach deserve careful consideration, weighing the possible outcomes and risks involved. Diversification requires careful investigation because of the risk of investing in unknown markets. A horizontal diversification strategy may include expanding products into similar markets in order to appeal to existing customers.

With regard to market segmentation strategy, we have seen above that experienced tourists are less sensitive to the media portrayal of destination image. Thus, following behaviour segmentation strategy by targeting the experienced tourist segment can be an effective crisis preparedness strategy.

Regarding crisis mitigation and preparedness, organisations must consider two issues. First, both mitigation and preparedness strategies must be incorporated into the strategic management of organisations and made part of long-term planning. Second, the issue of risk reduction arises. When destinations suffer from chronic political crises and unrest, serious consideration needs to be given to suspending or permanently removing them from the inventory. India, Fiji and Thailand fall into this category.

Crisis responses employed by trade organisations could be categorized as operational, marketing and financial. Operational responses relate to customer service, faster communication and strong relationships with all relevant trade organisations and stakeholders. Customer service remains paramount, because it enables trade organisations to retain their clients' loyalty. Such customers are more likely to purchase from those trade organisations which have provided them with good customer service in the past, particularly during disruptive events.

Another aspect of crisis response is marketing response, which involves suspending marketing of affected destinations or enhancing the marketing efforts of those unaffected. Finally, as tourism organisations are economically affected by political crises, a financial response is needed.

The crisis response phase may concentrate on three aspects:

(1) Businesses require inside information from trusted sources. Businesses should have, or develop, a set of direct and highly-trusted relationships, enabling them to access knowledge beyond local media sources, either more directly through contacts at destinations or with more immediacy through social media. Such access can also help reassure customers of their trustworthiness. The way to build these

special, informative relationships is best achieved through social media, email or direct telephone contact.

(2) Simple, clear messages to customers are important. A code of conduct or set of promises could be established. This could be built into promotional material and documents, so that customers know their service provider has thought about likely troublesome situations, and has clear response plans.

(3) Crises are global in nature, so in order to implement immediate responses effectively, the question of time difference needs to be addressed. When a crisis occurs and tourist-generating countries are in a different time zone, this invariably renders the situation more challenging for tourism managers. This issue should be incorporated into crisis management.

Crisis recovery strategies primarily focus on marketing. Collaborative efforts between stakeholders both in affected destinations and tourist-generating regions can abbreviate the crisis recovery period. The last stage is organisational learning, which, as discussed previously, must be integrated into the present study.

A FRAMEWORK OF POLITICAL CRISIS RESPONSES

The framework demonstrates the role of tourism in the destination region and the tourist-generating region. When a political crisis occurs, stakeholders feel the impact in both regions. The ramifications of crisis vary depending upon the type of crisis (e.g. war, civil war, coup, terrorism, riots/protests/unrest, strikes), its origin, the management of it, and cultural differences. The image of a destination is immediately damaged by a crisis, and as it deteriorates, stakeholders lose confidence. Crisis information is conveyed to stakeholders in both the destination and the tourist-generating regions. Those in the latter area include tourists and trade organisations (tour operators, travel agents, tourism consultants and destination organisations) who respond to the effects by implementing strategic management initiatives.

This framework divides political crisis management into five stages. The first stage occurs when organisations prepare for possible effects of political crises. This is done by applying *mitigation strategies* (e.g. risk reduction, perception assessment, and insurance coverage) and *preparedness strategies* during the pre-event stage (e.g. diversification, marketing segmentation and strengthening crisis communication). When a political crisis befalls a destination, the *management response* is implemented to deal with the immediate effects. However, those responses vary.

Six factors influence the crisis response:

1. the degree of violence;

2. the duration of the crisis;

3. the characteristics of the affected destination;

4. the timing of the political crisis;

5. the coincidence of several crises at once;

6. the level of media coverage of the situation.

The implementation of crisis response procedures can itself be divided into three perspectives: operational response, marketing response and financial response. The operational response considers customer service, expedited communication and strong relationships with stakeholders. The marketing response includes the strategies of marketing suspension, enhancing marketing of unaffected destinations and marketing substitute products. Financial evaluation is used to assess the financial consequences of the crisis.

After the crisis has passed, crisis recovery is implemented in order to restore stakeholder confidence, which can be achieved if stakeholders and governments collaborate effectively. Recovery strategies may include online marketing, trust-building, public relations campaigns and collaborative efforts between stakeholders.

The last stage occurs when crisis management strategies are *reviewed* and improvements are made for future political crises; feedback is also dispersed to tourism stakeholders in tourist-generating regions.

The next figure demonstrates three important factors in times of political crisis: the political crises' impacts, destination image and political crisis management. As a political crisis affects the image of a destination, implementation of crisis management can reduce the adverse effects while restoring stakeholder confidence.

Four steps are required to understand how to apply the political crisis response framework to current political crisis application:

Classifying political crises by using the political crisis classification model,

understanding the characteristics of a political crisis,

evaluations of the impacts of a political crisis

applying political crisis strategies according to the characteristics and impacts of a particular crisis.

Examining political crises in 2013, different crises result in different impacts and implications. This section addresses how the political crisis response framework can be applied to real situations in the year 2013 such as the ongoing crisis in Egypt, the Kenyan attack, the chronic political protests in Thailand, and the United States federal government shutdown.

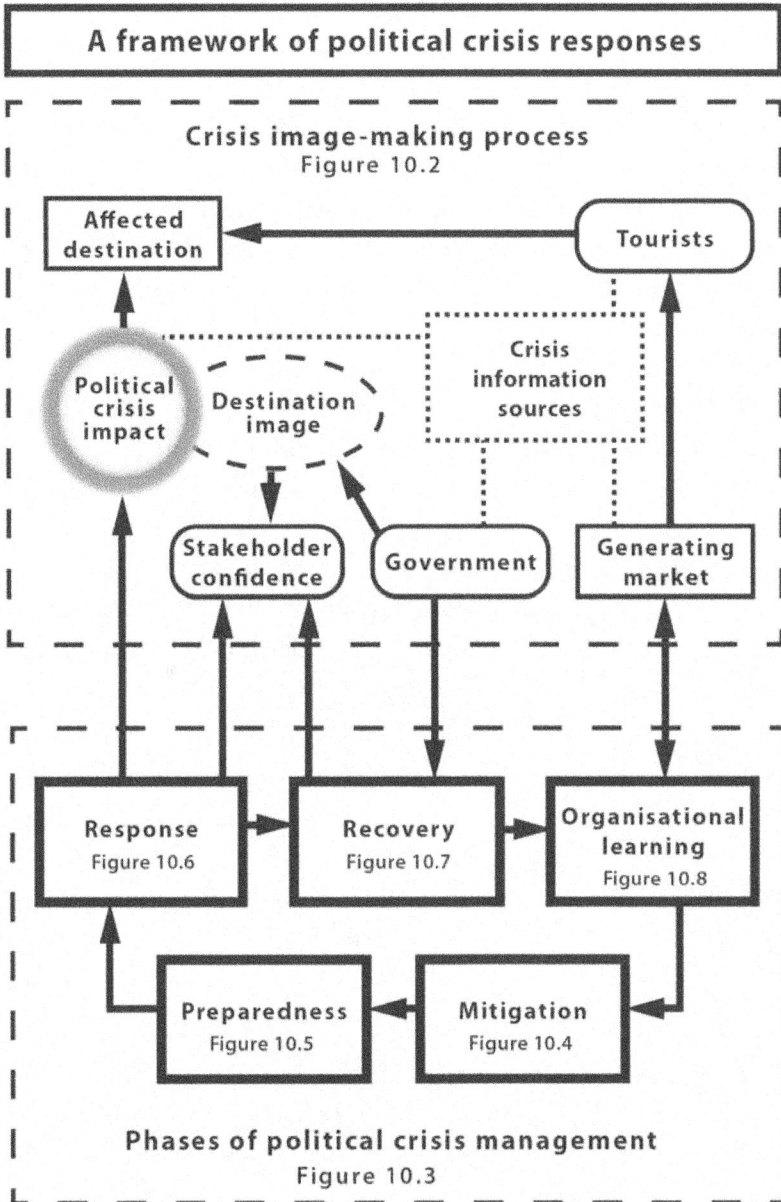

FIGURE 10.9

SUMMARY

Problems with political crises affecting destinations have markedly increased with the growth of tourism, particularly in emerging economies. This framework specifically addresses political crisis management as opposed to crises originating from other causes, such as natural disasters, as they create a different set of problems, ranging from the perceived image of a destination to governmental cooperation which may not be available or functional in the context of political crises.

This classification model is designed to assist the tourism industry in outlining the various types of political crisis. A number of methods and techniques have been identified to deal with the repercussions of political crises according to the different phases of the crisis cycle.

While a political crisis management plan is clearly beneficial for tourism managers, many organisations do not currently have such plans in place. They should urgently consider putting this right.

CHAPTER 11

EXAMPLE OF APPLICATION OF THE FRAMEWORK TO FOUR POLITICAL CRISES

To make it easier to understand the parallels and the differences between the four types of political crises, the four examples used are placed in each of the four quadrants of the classification model shown in the previous chapter (Figure 10.1).

SYNOPSIS

Type: Violent ephemeral crisis
Kenya: terror attack (September 2013)
On 21 September 2013, a terror attack on a shopping mall in Nairobi lasting four days left 72 people dead. As a consequence of the attack, the affected tourist areas also included areas within 60 kilometres of the Kenya-Somali border.

Type: Violent enduring crisis
Egypt: Revolution and crisis (2011 – present)
The year after the Arab Spring of 2010, the Egyptian Revolution of 2011 started a cycle of crises rising to a succession of violent incidents in 2013 and 2014. The affected destinations include Cairo and much of the Egyptian mainland as well as the Sanai peninsula, notably Sharm el-Sheikh in 2015.

BLOOD ON THE BEACH

Type: Non-violent ephemeral crisis
USA: federal government shutdown - (October 2013)
The failure of Congress to pass the bill for fiscal year 2014 caused the government to shut down all non-essential activities. As a consequence, all tourist attractions on federal property, including national parks and The Statue of Liberty were closed for nearly two weeks.

Type: Non-violent enduring crisis
Thailand: political protests (2006 – present)
Since the coup d'état of 2006, Thailand has suffered from chronic political crises with frequent political protests. While some incidents lead to violence, with notably 80 death in 2010, most were non-violent and the overall crisis is classified as such. Bangkok has been periodically affected by the protests while all other tourist destinations have remained mostly unaffected. The southern provinces near the Malaysian border suffers from a violent enduring crisis that is unrelated to the political crisis.

IMPACT OF THE POLITICAL CRISES

Kenya - *Violent ephemeral crisis*
The perception of an unsafe image worsened including different segments of travellers such as leisure, VFRs and MICEs. Perception was further affected long-term due to political instability following the Kenyan crisis in 2008. Increased fear concerned tourism stakeholders resulting in greater financial impacts.

Egypt - *Violent enduring crisis*
The on-going political protests destroyed tourism economy due to loss of stakeholder confidence towards the destination as stakeholders are highly sensitive to protests involving violence. Declaration of state of emergency severely damaged the safety image of the country. The crisis deeply affects tourism business financially because of the enduring nature of the conflict.

USA - *Non-violent ephemeral crisis*
The closure of tourist sites such as the Statue of Liberty and national parks immediately affected tourist perception of the USA as a destination. However this incident was characterised as a rare one-time event. This political crisis therefore has not deteriorated tourists' and investors' perceptions of the destination. However this political crisis inevitably affected stakeholders financially.

Thailand - *Non-violent enduring crisis*
The enduring nature of the situation affects tourist and stakeholder confidence. Tourists and investors are less likely to consider Thailand as they are concerned about the possibility of renewed and sudden violent episodes.

POLITICAL CRISIS STRATEGIES - MITIGATION

Kenya - *Violent ephemeral crisis*
Evaluate the political situation and the potential recurrence of terrorism. Select destinations where insurance coverage is maintained.

USA - *Non-violent ephemeral crisis*
Suggest re-scheduling of travel to the US during the 1-17 October 2013 period with no further action required.

Egypt - *Violent enduring crisis*
Avoid sending tourists to Egypt. Even though the city of Sharm El-Sheikh is not affected, the situation remains uncertain. If tourists nevertheless wish to travel to the area, check insurance coverage and select airlines with extensive networks in the region to facilitate potential tourist repatriation.

Thailand - *Non-violent enduring crisis*
While the small-scale and non-violent nature of the protests in 2013 means that they are, in themselves, not a cause of concern, the history and unpredictability of the potential development of events dictates that tourism stakeholders pay close attention to the situation to be able to respond promptly to any change. Insurance coverage for Thailand is provided except for the four southern provinces subject to the FCO travel advisory.

POLITICAL CRISIS STRATEGIES - PREPAREDNESS

Kenya - *Violent ephemeral crisis*
Diversify products to other destinations in the region. Communication channels need to be maintained, especially with tourists who are on location in remote areas.

Egypt - *Violent enduring crisis*
As the Egyptian crisis is an enduring one, trade organisations must diversify their destinations in the region. Alternatively, target tourists seeking to travel dangerously or those who wish to visit post-conflict areas.

USA - *Non-violent ephemeral crisis*
Strengthening communication in times of crisis could help tourism organisations.

Thailand - *Non-violent enduring crisis*
Target experienced travellers who are less likely to be sensitive to political conflict news or target travellers who have been in Thailand previously.
Diversify product portfolio to include neighbouring countries such as Malaysia and Singapore. In case the protests turn violent, tourists can alter their plan to fly through Singapore or Kuala Lumpur.

POLITICAL CRISIS STRATEGIES - RESPONSE

Kenya - *Violent ephemeral crisis*
As soon as the news of the attack spread, tourism organisations immediately located their clients who were in Kenya to keep them informed of the situation and offer them the choice to evacuate or remain in the area. Then contact hotels to ascertain clients' safety. Update clients with impending travel.

Egypt - *Violent enduring crisis*
Following the declaration of the state of emergency, contact customers who are currently in destination to give them the choice to evacuate or remain in the area. Trade organisations market substitute products with similar characteristics, such as Morocco.

USA - *Non-violent ephemeral crisis*
Have alternative plans in place to visit state and local tourist spots on those days federally managed sites are closed. Such plans could be available when access to these sites is disrupted by other causes, such as weather conditions or public demonstrations.

Thailand - *Non-violent enduring crisis*
Inform clients who are at the affected destination, but it is not necessary to evacuate clients out of the protest areas or the country as the small-scale protests are localised and non-violent.
The Thai government issues regular press releases to keep stakeholders informed.

POLITICAL CRISIS STRATEGIES - RECOVERY

Kenya - *Violent ephemeral crisis*
Kenyan government needs to re-establish confidence by effectively communicating the ephemeral and localised nature of the event. Invite public figures to visit the country to reinforce the safety image of the country.

Egypt - *Violent enduring crisis*
Egyptian government invites foreign journalists to visit the tourist destinations; communicate that Egypt is now safe.

USA - *Non-violent ephemeral crisis*
US government issued a press release updating the situations to normal; all federally-managed tourist sites reopened.

Thailand - *Non-violent enduring crisis*
Promotional campaign by national airline (Thai Airways). Also campaigns to promote major events such as football friendlies with British clubs and golf tournaments attracting leading players.

POLITICAL CRISIS STRATEGIES – ORGANISATIONAL LEARNING

Kenya - *Violent ephemeral crisis*
While tourist attacks occur without notice, foretelling signs and geolocation awareness can mitigate the risks. For example, Al-Shabaab is a terrorist group based in Somalia where the Kenyan army has a UN sanctioned policing role.

Egypt - *Violent enduring crisis*
Due to on-going political crises, inform clients of potential trouble before travelling to Egypt.

USA - *Non-violent ephemeral crisis*
The US government shutdown is an example of the potential consequences of crises that generally remain within the political sphere in politically stable countries. Tourism managers must consider the potential consequences of political crises even in politically stable climates.

Thailand - *Non-violent enduring crisis*
Political crises in Thailand can break out at any time because of the unstable nature of the country's political situation requiring tourism organisations to keep well-informed of current events.

CHAPTER 12

EFFECTS OF A CRISIS ON ALTERNATIVE DESTINATIONS

Political crises can have a quite different effect on destinations elsewhere which offer similar attractions to tourists, even if they are not in the same region, as tourists and operators need to find somewhere else to send their clients. While this creates a surge in demand for alternative destinations, this is not necessarily beneficial, as the shift in demand is usually sudden and unplanned for. Consequently, alternative destinations are faced with similar disruptions to those in tourist-generating markets, as demand shifts very suddenly at the onset of a political crisis elsewhere in the world.

Just like travel agents and operators, tourism organisations in the alternative destinations need to consider their own marketing response, which may be scaled up or down depending upon their capacity to accommodate and service an unplanned surge in demand.

As with other consumer products, when a destination's appeal is diminished by a crisis, the tourists who intended to visit that destination still want to buy. They do not stay at home. They choose another destination which either offers similar features or happens to be next on their wish list.

In the 1980s, Thailand became the benefiting alternative destination to Sri Lanka after the latter entered a long period of civil war. The more recent crisis in Egypt caused the loss of more than 5 million visitors compared with its peak in 2010. The magnitude of the shift can be huge. To put the Egyptian loss in perspective, the country lost more tourists than the Philippines received in 2013 and nearly as many as Brazil did. If we add the loss from the crisis in Syria, once the third most popular destination in the Middle East region, which amounts to well over 5 million visitors, that means that more than 10 million visitors to the Middle East shifted to other destinations. Most of them, some 7 million, were lost to places outside the region, with only the UAE gaining – it received almost 3 million visitors over that period.

Greek and Turkish destinations are the obvious alternatives to Egypt, as they both offer the combination of beach resorts and major historical sites from antiquity. Over the 2010-2013 period, Greece and Turkey both saw tourism grow by 20%, far above the 12% average in their region. That difference of 8%, or about 3.5 million extra visitors, is very likely explained in the most part by Egypt's loss of 5 million visitors. The chart below clearly shows the mirror patterns of Egypt and Greece throughout that period, and the smaller, but nonetheless noticeable, influence on Turkey.

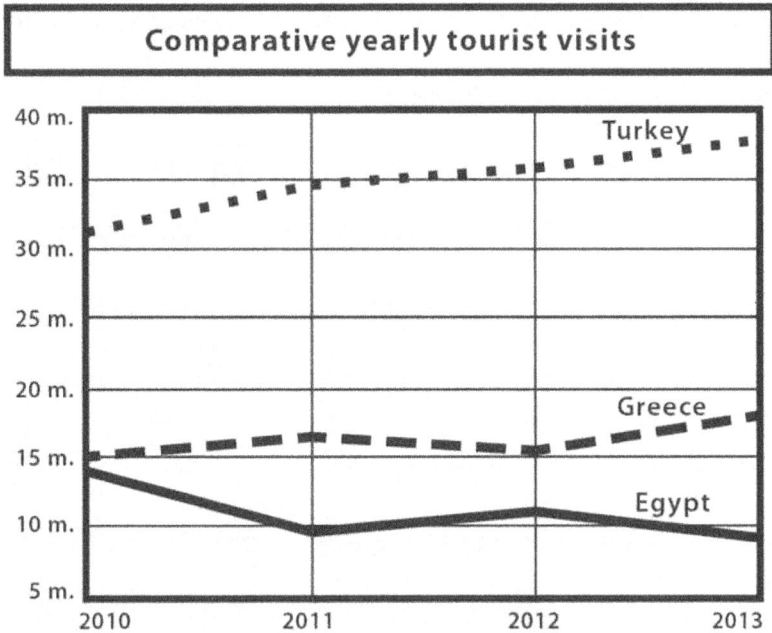

FIGURE 12.1

If the destination's major interest is cultural or historical, like that of a UNESCO world heritage site, the alternative destination choice may be in a completely different part of the world, as long as it is within the initial budget. For a European tourist, Greece and Turkey are the obvious alternatives to Egypt, as we have seen above, but for a Middle Eastern tourist, the alternatives may be Jordan, Lebanon or Iran, provided these destinations are not affected by conflicts or crises themselves.

The alternatives to some destinations may lie halfway around the world. Consider Angkor Wat in Cambodia for either a European or an American tourist; Machu Picchu in Peru would be a likely choice, considering the similarities in historical significance and visual scale, and it is roughly equal in travel time and cost from either Europe or North America.

163

If the destination's main attraction is beach and sun, then alternative destinations are not so obvious, as the tourist's choice will be influenced by other considerations relative to their own lifestyle. The successive crises in Thailand, for example, caused a cycle of chronic downturns and upswings in its tourism industry. At first glance, Malaysia would seem to be the obvious alternative destination, yet the International Tourist Arrival data for Malaysia from UNWTO does not show any significant upturns when Thailand has a crisis year. Instead, Malaysia has had a slow but steady growth for the last ten years, apparently unaffected by the ups and downs of its northern neighbour's tourism. Bali or Vietnam are perceived as better alternative destinations to Thailand than Malaysia, even though Malaysia has very similar beaches to Thailand because other lifestyle considerations give an advantage to Bali and Vietnam.

Even a destination as remote from Thailand as Spain is likely be a strong alternative, as they are surprisingly similar in tourist features and conveniences and share a common appeal across generations.

In the Middle East region, the combined losses of Egypt and Syria of more than 10 million tourists probably contributed heavily to the strong growth of tourism in UAE, although they were picked up mainly from the regional market without gaining many visitors from other regions, as altogether the Middle East region had a net loss of nearly 7 million tourists. Over the same period, South-East Asia gained 23 million tourists, far more than any other region in the world, strongly contributing to the global growth of tourism. While the number of Chinese visitors has been growing strongly in South-East Asia, there remains a large difference, indicating that South-East Asia has also benefited from the loss of visitors to the Middle East.

THE 'WISH LIST BACKLOG'

There is a peculiar marketing aspect to tourism: a lost destination sale may not be lost, but postponed to a later date. Most people have a list, however informal, of places they want to visit at least once in their lifetime - Thailand, the Pyramids, New York, Machu Picchu etc. If their first choice is not currently available, it will remain on their list. Once a destination recovers from a crisis and becomes available again, a sort of 'wish list backlog' is unleashed, creating a surge of visitors who had postponed their visit to better times. The previous chart reflects this behaviour very well; it shows when Egypt recovered in 2012 from the 2011 crisis and Greece experienced a matching decline. Then when Egypt relapsed into crisis in 2013, Greece's numbers surged ahead again.

The backlog surge is typically absorbed within a year, as the year immediately following the recovery year often experiences a plateau or a shallow rate of growth. The years after that generally resume at the historic pace of growth. The dip of the crisis year is followed by a corresponding bump before resuming a normal pattern.

While the backlog surge is certainly good news for a recovering destination, it also creates a problem of excess demand for accommodation and logistics, particularly if some of the assets have been lost or damaged during the crisis, further limiting supply. The surge in demand can also drive prices up too high, causing further damage to the already battered destination image just as the destination is actively trying to rebuild its image in the aftermath of the crisis.

THE 'BOOM AND BUST' PROBLEM

The windfall of additional visitors to the alternative destination during a crisis at the affected destination is not necessarily all beneficial. If the alternative is already at optimum capacity, the unexpected surge of visitors may cause adverse effects, including excessive price increases or overcrowding at some attractions. This will affect all visitors, tarnishing the destination's image. Also, if the source of the surge is not correctly identified and understood as temporary, stakeholders may invest in further development based on projections derived from the higher number of visitors. This will lead to oversupply when the visitor pattern returns to normal. On the other hand, if the stakeholders do not act on the belief that the surge is temporary but the affected destination remains unavailable for years to come, as is the case with Syria, then saturation and overcrowding become difficult to alleviate and the alternative destination's image is further damaged instead of being enhanced.

CRISIS MANAGEMENT FOR ALTERNATIVE DESTINATIONS

Whether national and regional crises occur more frequently today than in the past is debatable, but their effect on tourism has unquestionably increased and become more frequent with the growth of global tourism. More destinations are affected more often than ever before. Consequently the growth pattern of alternative destinations is comparably disrupted by mostly unpredictable swings in visitor flow.

Tourism destinations should keep watch on crises and events that might affect similar destinations, as these events will indirectly affect them as well, no matter how geographically remote they may be. The first step is to compile a watch list of destinations, ordered by the likelihood and magnitude of visitor shift to the alternative destination a crisis or event might cause. Taking the example of Greece; visitor statistics of recent years show that Egypt is the destination most likely to affect it in the greatest numbers.

As crises and events are, by their nature, mostly unpredictable, or at best happen at very short notice, the alternative destinations have limited ability to react and prepare for the unplanned surge of visitors. Contingency management will also be different if the destination has spare capacity, such as in times of economic downturns, or is already at its peak. Obviously, if there is spare capacity, promotion and marketing should be stepped up and the tourists who initially intended to visit the affected destination should be targeted. On the other hand, if the destination is already at peak capacity, promotion would promptly be scaled down or revised to focus on areas which are less likely to receive these additional visitors. One should keep in mind that as outlined above, an unexpected surge in tourism could well bring difficult problems along with the potential benefits.

CHAPTER 13

CONCLUSIONS

The theme of this book, managing political crises in the tourism industry, underscores the mutually dependent relationship between tourism and politics. The influence of politics on tourism, including international relations, public administration and public policies, is often so profound as to fundamentally affect the long-term success or failure of a destination. However, while tourism is a major contributor to the GNP of many countries, particularly emerging economies, its influence on politics is small compared to other major industries and consequently tends to be relegated to a passive role in policy-making.

There is an intimate link between politics, crises and tourism. The primary requirement of tourists is not relaxation or culture but political stability and associated safety. A destination located in a politically unstable area is greatly affected by political crises, leading tourists to seek substitute destinations elsewhere. When a political crisis devastates a destination, it may be a long time before its image is restored and confidence among all stakeholders is regained. This is in part due to the fragility of a destination's image; in turn, stakeholders, including hoteliers, airlines, tour operators and travel companies, suffer financial damage. In some severe political crises, such as war and civil war, the economy of the affected destination can find itself so deeply affected that the tourism industry is unable to recover. Stakeholders must employ strategies that can help to restore destination image and tourist demand in the aftermath of a political crisis. Understanding the concepts of politics and crises with regards to tourism is at the foundation of this book.

Different political crises cause distinct impacts on tourism destinations and organizations. For example, the Egyptian Revolution destroyed the country's tourism industry, while the prolonged Thai political crisis has created an enduring image of politically instability which has resulted in a loss of confidence. The tourism industry needs different crisis management strategies for each distinct phase of a crisis.

The perception of trade organisations is of critical importance if we are to appreciate the impacts of political crises. These organizations are critical in the process of crisis management of a destination's image. The perceptions of stakeholders in trade organisations across tourism sectors relative to the effects of political crises bring diverse opinions and perceptions. Of particular concern are safety and security issues caused by loss of confidence, fear of loss and lack of future confidence towards the affected destination, especially those with a chronic history of political crises.

The research and interviews on which this book is based provide ample insight into the variable effects of political crises based on particular situations and perceptions of them. The impacts of political crises have been comprehensively categorised into the following effects: the perception effect, the financial effect and the aftermath. The influencing factors include the ripple effect, the coinciding effect and the spillover effect. These effects are further classified based upon the time lapse of events (e.g. immediate, short-term and long-term). The perception effect, a destination's image and stakeholder confidence are all key factors in political crisis management.

If proper crisis management is undertaken during the response phase, impacts in the short and long terms can be mitigated, reducing the recovery period. Unfortunately, as both the academic and the business literature on tourism lack essential preparedness strategies including diversification and behavioural segmentation, stakeholders have few references readily available to them to implement tactical strategies in crises management. The emphasis of this book is on management response specifically to address this issue.

Crisis recovery strategies are necessary to both the private and the public sector. Government plays an integral role for crisis management during the recovery phase, while private organisations, including tourism organisations, the media and tour operators also contribute significantly to shortening the crisis recovery phase.

The framework of political crises responses is intended to provide knowledge and reference to the tourism industry and will assist stakeholders in better understanding the dynamics of political crises and their unique impacts on tourism destinations.

PRE-EVENT STAGE: MITIGATION AND PREPAREDNESS

The pre-event stage includes actions to prevent or mitigate the effects of potential political crises in future. Management during this phase includes the implementation of a crisis mitigation strategy and a crisis preparedness strategy. Such preparedness strategies include diversification of tourism products, market segmentation and strengthening communication. Different types of crises should be classified within such a framework, such as natural disasters or political crises, in order to support the effectiveness of the crisis management plan.

Examples of this phase can be seen in the chronic political crises taking place in Thailand, where operators attempted to mitigate the risks of potential crises by organising tours that bypassed the affected city of Bangkok, shifting focus instead to other areas of the country. The operators also cultivated strong relationships with their business partners, such as airlines and hotels at the affected destinations, in order to ensure support would be available if a crisis were to occur.

Crisis management can be incorporated into strategic management in two ways. First, by proactive planning and strategy formulation by environmental scanning, issues analysis, scenario planning, strategic forecasting and risk analysis, and secondly by planning for scanning and issue analysis, making contingency and emergency plans or adjusting any other plans for potential crises.

EMERGENCY AND INTERMEDIATE STAGES: RESPONSE

During the emergency phase, a crisis operational response strategy needs to be implemented if a high degree of violence is involved; organisations immediately evacuate their customers from destinations where such situations occur, while short-term planning also requires attention. Adjusting marketing and financial strategies at this time ensures post-crisis business continuity and recovery in the subsequent stages.

At this stage, an operational response is first implemented according to the effects of political crises, especially where people are at the affected destination and are consequently directly affected by the crisis.

The main objectives of the emergency phase are twofold. Firstly, to care for customers currently at the affected destination, and secondly, to immediately activate communication and gather crisis information while conveying appropriate messages to customers, business partners and other stakeholders. Moreover, crisis management needs to include a coherent management response and offer accurate information to customers. Necessary action must be taken, such as evacuation procedures, emergency accommodation, distribution of medical supplies and health services.

Collaboration becomes crucial at this stage among all stakeholder, such as internal communication between employees and managers and external communications between customers, tourism boards, government agencies and the media. In the case of the 2011 Egyptian revolution, operators immediately located all their customers in the country and implemented their evacuation plans to fly them out. As in this case, necessary action needs to be taken immediately during the emergency phase of a crisis.

Continued from the emergency phase is the intermediate phase, where short-term crisis management responses such as marketing and financial responses are implemented to alleviate the effects of political crises. The strategies implemented during this phase exist to help an organisation minimise any effects that have already occurred. Marketing responses, such as suspending destination marketing, are effective, as are financial responses such as implementing cost control in operations departments and auditing to ensure business continuity.

The emergency and immediate phases are critical in terms of crisis management response and must be implemented accordingly in the operational, marketing and financial sectors of an organisation. Proper crisis management response can reduce the short-term and long-term effects of political crises while expediting the crisis recovery phase.

LONG-TERM RECOVERY PHASE

The long-term phase is when crisis recovery strategies can be set in motion. The main goal immediately following a crisis is to minimise the negative effects, prevent further depletion of confidence and restore stakeholder confidence as soon as possible. In the long term, however, the main strategy centres on the restoration of the destination image. Reviving the image of the destination to the travelling public at large while restoring media confidence and communication are singularly important for the long-term health of the destination. Reassessment of infrastructure (which may have suffered damage), rehabilitation of affected areas and restoration of tourist and investor confidence are all needed together. During this phase, the action which must be taken includes destination marketing, niche marketing, enhancement of public relations and publicity. Full collaboration between stakeholders in the tourism industry is requisite to recovery in this period; stakeholders in tourist-generating regions should establish strong relationships with those in affected destinations to facilitate a full recovery effort.

RESOLUTION: ORGANISATIONAL LEARNING

Finally, the resolution phase allows organisations to evaluate the effects of political crises on their organisations and re-evaluate their strategies, if necessary, for future events. Certain destinations such as India, Fiji and Thailand suffer from political crisis lifecycles. This makes the evaluation, implementation and monitoring of crisis management essential. Flexibility is needed to allow for optimal development and evolution.

The benefits of the political crisis response framework are not limited to tourism organisations but extend to governments in both affected destinations and tourist-generating regions; the framework addresses aspects of a government's reaction towards an affected destination following a political crisis, such as diplomacy and international relations, which can affect all trade organisations. For example, following the 2008 Mumbai attack, the Indian Government's diplomacy and international relations with Pakistan deteriorated when the Indian Prime Minister stated that the terrorists originated from Pakistan, an allegation that caused tension and disturbed trade between the two nations. The Indian government's reaction affected trade organisations in India and Pakistan, as well as other tourist-generating regions, which send tourists across their borders. Chronic ceasefire violations along the India-Pakistan border in the Jammu and Samba districts have further ignited tensions between the two countries.

It is clear that political crises affect relations with neighbouring countries, as in the case of Myanmar. As tourism developed recently there, some regions of the country remain restricted due to the ongoing conflicts in the Shan, Karen, Mon and Kachin states; this has resulted in border restrictions between Myanmar and China, as well as increased safety concerns for tourists in the border areas of Thailand, Laos, and China.

The Foreign and Commonwealth Office (FCO) travel advisories have an impact on trade organisations in tourist-generating regions, tourism destinations and local economies affected by crises. The effects of FCO travel advisories on the tourism sector are magnified, as the insurance sector safeguards its financial exposure by limiting or declining coverage to destinations cited in FCO advisories. These advisories are the single most important consideration taken into account by trade organisations when discouraging clients from travelling to affected destinations. The economic impact of travel advisories in both the tourist-generating regions and the affected destinations remains an open question. Perhaps governments in these places, as well as government departments such as the Foreign and Commonwealth Office, should consider this framework to better understand the economic implications of their diplomacy, public statements and actions pertaining to travel in and around affected areas.

The political crisis classification model presented in this book is primarily intended to help trade organisations understand and classify political crises in order to respond to their impact. However, potential users of this model are not limited to trade organisations; government, media, stakeholders further afield, insurance, finance, transport, construction, and others can all benefit. Affected destinations' governments can apply the political crisis classification model to develop diplomatic responses according to each crisis type; the governments in generating markets can use this model to assess the larger impact of crisis before issuing travel advisories.

APPENDIX A

THE INTERVIEWEES

The source material for this book included in-depth, face-to-face interviews with 20 tourism experts, all high-level executives from different sectors of the UK tourism industry. These interviews were originally undertaken in the research of the thesis that was at the origin of the book. The interview fieldwork procedure for this study posed a number of challenges. Several key issues emerged from the interviews which revealed variable levels of understanding of political crises, their effects, and strategies to cope with them.

Destination organisations include tourism boards that represent and promote their country or region's tourism destinations *vis-à-vis* international offices (e.g. the Tourism Authority of Thailand in London). Tourism consultants are experts who offer special knowledge to tour operators and travel agents and are based in the UK. Some aspects of the tourism consultants' services include advising tour operators and travel agents on regulatory aspects of ATOL, ABTA and IATA licences, discussing with individual companies whether to market certain destinations, and consulting over which strategies should be applied to certain destinations to be competitive in the market.

Travel agents act as intermediaries or brokers between consumers and tour operators. Their income is derived from the commission earned by selling travel products on behalf of operators. Travel agents may assemble products into individual or customised travel programmes, but they do not organise tours; they sell tourism products and services provided by others. This category tends to carry less responsibility. However when political crises occur, they directly contact clients at the affected destination; they will not typically give client contact information to operators.

Tour operators interact with tourists and suppliers (e.g. hoteliers, airlines), making them an excellent source of information for this study. They represent the majority of the interviewees in this study. Tour operators maintain contact with both clients and travel agents while keeping both parties informed at all times. Some have established subsidiaries at particular destinations for the purpose of enhancing travel services; these companies are mainly the larger tour corporations. Small and medium-sized enterprises normally coordinate with destination management organisations or ground handlers, to provide services such as transportation. Tour operators are also responsible for solving problems for tourists whenever political crises occur. Different companies adopt different procedures.

www.ingramcontent.com/pod-product-compliance
Lightning Source LLC
Chambersburg PA
CBHW060452280326
41933CB00014B/2737